Y0-EES-736

658.0094 B623e 1997
Bloom, Helen.
Euromanagement : a new
style for the global market

WITHDRAWN

Date Due

NOV 27 1999			
OCT 06 2000			
DEC 13 2001			
JUL 25 2002			
MAY 09 2003			
APR 26 2003			

BRODART, CO. Cat. No. 23-233-003 Printed in U.S.A.

EURO
MANAGEMENT

THE EURO BUSINESS PUBLISHING NETWORK

The Euro Business Publishing Network (EBPN) is a consortium of leading European business publishers whose members are

Kogan Page, UK
Les Editions d'Organisation, France
Verlag Moderne Industrie, Germany
Franco Angeli, Italy
Liber, Sweden
Deusto, Spain

The members of the EBPN work closely together to publish leading edge business and management books from authors throughout Europe.

Euromanagement is also published in the French language under the title, *L'art du management europeen,* by Les Editions d'Organisation of 1 Rue Thenard, 75240 Paris Cedex 05, France.

EURO MANAGEMENT

A New Style for the Global Market

Helen Bloom • Roland Calori
Philippe de Woot

First published in 1994

Reprinted 1994, 1997

Apart from any fair dealing for the purposes of research or private study, or criticism or review, as permitted under the Copyright, Designs and Patents Act, 1988, this publication may only be reproduced, stored or transmitted, in any form or by any means, with the prior permission in writing of the publishers, or in the case of reprographic reproduction in accordance with the terms of licences issued by the Copyright Licensing Agency. Enquiries concerning reproduction outside those terms should be sent to the publishers at the undermentioned address:

Kogan Page Limited
120 Pentonville Road
London N1 9JN

© The European Round Table of Industrialists and Groupe ESC Lyon, 1994

British Library Cataloguing in Publication Data

A CIP record for this book is available from the British Library.

ISBN 0 7494 1207 0

Typeset by Books Unlimited (Nottm), Sutton-in-Ashfield, NG17 1AL

Printed and bound in Great Britain by
Biddles Ltd, Guildford and King's Lynn

Contents

Foreword 9

Introduction 11

    The aim of the study   11
    Participants in the study   12
    European Round Table of Industrialists (ERT)   15
    Groupe ESC Lyon   16

1 How Europeans view management 17

    The evolving European management model   18
    The challenge of change   20
    Social change   21
    The response to change   22

2 A changing order 25

    A new world order   26
    The importance of balance   27
    Maintaining balance in turbulence   28

3 The European view of the world 31

    Echoes of humanism   31
    Contradictions   33
    The desire to survive   35

A summarizing view   35
A cultural heritage   37

4 Managing international diversity 39

The pros and cons of diversity   40
Who has the know-how?   43
Understanding and respecting other cultures   46
A 'glocal' approach to the Single Market   50
Integrating diversity   53

5 Social responsibility 55

A broader purpose   56
The company as part of society   57
The price of a social role   59
Links with government   60
Long-term thinking   62
Constraints on British firms   64
Maintaining an equilibrium   66

6 Internal negotiations 67

Labour relations   68
The northern system   70
The Latin system   71
The British variation   72
Towards a more united approach   73

7 Attitudes to human resources 75

Japanese attitudes   75
Contrasts with America   76
Individuality and conformity   77
Mistrust of authority   78
Quality of life   79

Learning from Japan   80
'Female' characteristics   81

8 Women in business   83

Scandinavia leads Europe   84
Ability more than ambition   85
Glass ceilings   86
Combining career and family   87
A generation seeking balance   89
'Macho' is outmoded   89
'Equality' must mean 'equal'   91
Ahead of the rest   91

9 Management with leadership   93

Management   93
Leadership   94
Japanese CEOs manage more than lead   97
Systems are not enough   99
Tools and rules   100
Balancing systems and sense   102
Leading *and* managing   103

10 Competing worldwide   105

Customers and quality   106
A world outlook   109
Global markets   110
Not either/or, but both   111

11 Future challenges   113

The industry/finance interface   114
Balancing social responsibility with competitiveness   115
Making the most of the Single Market   116

8 Euromanagement

    Building in flexibility   116
    Quality in people as well as products and processes   117
    Customer service at every level   118
    Eastern Europe   119

12 Euromanagement skills   121

    The capacity to change   122
    An open mindset   122
    The ability to learn from others   123
    An entrepreneurial spirit   124
    Communication skills   125
    Business schools for the Single Market   126

13 Reconciling forces   131

    A European management model   131
    Reconciling contradictory forces   132

Appendix: The participants in the study   135

Foreword

Do we Europeans have our own special ways of running a business? Do we differ in this respect from our principal competitors — the Americans and the Japanese? Is there a *European* management model? These are difficult questions, and ones which deserve consideration.

More than 50 chairmen, chief executives and company directors of some of the largest companies in Europe were asked to reflect on these questions. This book summarizes their views. They converge sufficiently to convince us of a fundamental reality: the culture and history of Europe have deeply influenced our management philosophy, standards and practices.

There are also many paradoxes revealed in this book. One is that the prime characteristic of Europe is its diversity. There is not one management style in Europe, but several: the North is different to the South, and within those categories there are more distinctions. Yet our common European characteristics overcome these differences the moment we compare ourselves to the United States or Japan.

Another paradox involves a company's 'social responsibilities'. References to the social market economic model run through this book like a *leitmotif*. Most of the directors interviewed emphasized the social dimensions of business and the fact that for them profit is not the sole aim of a company.

As my colleague François Cornélis has said 'The people who work in our companies are part of a very old civilization and they expect us, their directors, to behave in a civilized manner.' This is very true. Yet global competition and the current economic crisis have hit us extremely hard, obliging us to restructure our companies. This has led to the elimination of jobs, and even to massive lay-offs.

Will the social aspects of European business management survive the current crisis? Personally, I think they will — on condition that they adapt. Our social market model will then evolve in line with its main themes and values.

This book shows that the dynamics of European integration are accelerating the emergence of a European management model. The creation of a single market of 350 million consumers constitutes a major challenge for our companies: they will have to widen their perspectives and horizons to the breadth of the continent, which will be the new springboard for a global strategy. Our companies are living through a common experience of profound change and meeting very similar problems and opportunities. No doubt this will influence their management styles and make them more similar. It is clear that the vision and the European policies of companies will shape the elements of the European management model which is emerging.

This European management model will not eliminate the national models. Rather it will add a dimension to them: a common way of being European.

This book is published under the auspices of the European Round Table of Industrialists (ERT). It is the result of an initiative by the ERT Working Group on Education, which was taken up very dynamically by the Lyon Graduate School of Business.

During this period when Europe is being constructed, it is especially important to be conscious of our cultural backgrounds and their influence on our management styles. If we become more conscious of our European characteristics — of their strengths, of their weaknesses, of their ambiguities — we will be able to use the best of them to enhance our international comparative advantages.

That is why the message of this book is addressed to all directors and managers who work in Europe, as well as to the business and management schools which prepare those who in the future will be responsible for the international performance of our companies.

Bertrand Collomb
Chairman and Chief Executive Officer
Lafarge Coppée

Introduction

THE AIM OF THE STUDY

This book is based on a study which aimed to determine whether there are common characteristics of good management across western Europe, and how knowledge of them can be used to improve management education and development.

The study was initiated in 1992 by Bertrand Collomb, Chairman and CEO of Lafarge Coppée and then Chairman of the European Round Table Working Group on Education, and Bruno Dufour, Director-General of the Groupe ESC Lyon — the Lyon Graduate School of Business. Research and interviews for the study were carried out by members of the faculty and staff of the Groupe ESC Lyon.

More than 50 chairmen, chief executive officers, vice-presidents, directors and human resource managers of 35 international companies based in 14 European countries participated in the study by giving interviews. Most of them were European and Members of the European Round Table, or top managers in their companies. But to give an 'outsider's' view the group also included American and Japanese managers of European operations of major US and Japanese companies. A list of those interviewed is given below. Fuller descriptions of them and their companies are in the Appendix.

PARTICIPANTS IN THE STUDY[*]

Agfa-Gevaert	André Leysen, Chairman of the Supervisory Board
Amorim Group	Américo Amorim, President
Austrian Industries	Paul F Roettig, Senior Vice President of Human Resources
Robert Bosch	Hans L Merkle, Managing Partner
British Petroleum	Robert Horton, former Chairman and CEO
BSN Group	Antoine Riboud, Chairman and CEO
	Daniel Lefort, Director-General of Human Resources
The Coca-Cola Company	Ralph H Cooper, Senior Vice-President and President of European Community Group
Daimler-Benz	Claudia Schlossberger, Senior Manager in Development Corporate Executive
Fiat	Umberto Agnelli, Vice Chairman
	John Kirschen, Vice President of Fiat Europe
	Vittorio Tesio, Director of Personnel Planning and Management
	Laura Bonisconti, Head of the Group's Industrial Relations Research Office
Hewlett-Packard	André Breukels, Personnel Director of American Division
Hoechst	Justus Mische, Member of the Board in charge of Personnel
	Monika Düssel, Manager of International Affairs for the Central Office of the Board of Management

---

[*] Directors and managers from other companies also participated in the study, but asked not to be quoted and not to have their names included in this list.

Hoffmann-La Roche	Roland Berra, Head of Corporate Executive Resources
Itochu (UK)	Hiroshi Wakabayashi, Chief Executive
Lafarge Coppée	Bertrand Collomb, Chairman and CEO
Lyonnaise des Eaux-Dumez	Jérôme Monod, Chairman and Président Directeur-Général
	Marc Fornacciari, Director of Planning
Nestlé	Helmut O Maucher, Chairman of the Board and CEO
The Nokia Group	Simo Vuorilehto, former CEO and Chairman of the Group Executive Board
	Kirsi-Marja Kuivalainen, Vice-President in charge of Human Resources
NTT Europe	Kageo Nakano, Managing Director
Petrofina	François Cornélis, CEO
Philips	Wisse Dekker, Chairman of the Supervisory Board
	Regina Matthijsen, Head of the International Industrial Relations Department
	Willem H J Guitink, Corporate Director of Management Training and Education
Pilkington	Sir Antony Pilkington, Chairman
Pirelli	Jacopo Vittorelli, former Deputy Chairman
	Gavino Manca, General Manager of Economic Affairs
	Silvia Petocchi, Personnel Manager for Pirelli's motor vehicle components divisions
Profilo Group	Jak V Kamhi, Chairman of the Board

Royal Dutch Shell	Ernest Van Mourik Broekman, Co-ordinator of Human Resources and Organization
Saint-Gobain	Jean-Louis Beffa, Chairman and CEO
Schneider Group	Didier Pineau-Valencienne, Président Directeur-Général
	Didier Guibert, Senior Vice President of Human Resources,
Siemens	Walter Schusser, Vice-President of Human Resources Management and Development
	Hans-Jörg Hörger, Corporate Director of Management Training
Société Générale de Belgique	Viscount Etienne Davignon, Chairman
Solvay	Baron Daniel Janssen, Chairman of the Executive Committee
Telefónica de España	José-Alberto Blanco Losada, Deputy General Director for Strategic Planning
Titan Cement Company	Theodore Papalexopoulos, Deputy Chairman
Total	Elisabeth Bukspan, Director of External Affairs
Trafalgar House	Brian Goldthorp, Director of Personnel, Trafalgar House Engineering Division
Unilever	Floris A Maljers, Chairman of the Board
Volvo	Pehr Gyllenhammar, former Executive Chairman

EUROPEAN ROUND TABLE OF INDUSTRIALISTS (ERT)

The European Round Table of Industrialists is composed of chairmen and chief executives of about 40 major multinational companies with their head office in Europe. They come from 17 European countries, represent a wide range of sectors of industry, and together have a combined turnover of some 500 billion ECU and more than three million employees worldwide. Membership of the ERT is personal and by invitation only.

The ERT was created in 1983 by Pehr Gyllenhammar of Volvo, Wisse Dekker of Philips and Umberto Agnelli of Fiat, with active support from two Commissioners of the European Community — Etienne Davignon and François-Xavier Ortoli, both of whom later joined the ERT after returning to industry. The initial ERT objective still holds true today: to strengthen Europe's economy and to improve its position as a global trading partner.

Over the past ten years the ERT has made many wide-ranging proposals for practical policies that contribute to the progress of the European economy. These are mostly published in ERT reports that are widely circulated in government, business and academic circles throughout Europe and further afield. Issues tackled include European infrastructure networks, indirect taxation, education and training, labour markets, North-South relations, communications technology and energy. Expert groups have also studied central and eastern Europe and European relations with the United States and Japan.

Above all, the ERT has exerted continuing pressure for the real achievement of the unified European market, and has repeatedly urged that the GATT Uruguay Round negotiations be successfully concluded. With the Maastricht Treaty now ratified, the ERT is actively promoting competitiveness and the reskilling of people of all ages and levels in order to achieve stronger economic growth and fuller employment. The widening as well as deepening of Europe is seen as a priority.

ERT members meet twice a year in plenary session to decide which major policy issues to take up, sometimes round the table, sometimes in policy groups that are chaired by ERT members and staffed by experts from ERT companies. When appropriate, ERT members will also meet the European Union Council President, the President and

Commissioners of the European Commission, and take ERT messages to the heads of national governments.

For younger managers in ERT companies, a continuing series of conferences and job-exchange programmes is available to develop the European directors of the future. In 1991–93 this programme was open to company managers from Poland, Hungary and the Czech and Slovak Republics.

A small Brussels-based Secretariat of eight permanent staff coordinates the work of the ERT.

GROUPE ESC LYON

The Groupe ESC Lyon is a French 'Grande Ecole' with an international scope which specializes in business education, management development and research. It defines its mission as working closely with companies to develop tomorrow's managers and entrepreneurs, to contribute to innovation in management methods, and to be a melting pot of European and international business cultures.

In business education, the Groupe offers eight programmes: ESC Lyon (the initial graduate degree in business education), the Cesma MBA (a postgraduate, post-experience degree), four specialized Master of Science degrees and two Doctoral programmes.

Two divisions of the Groupe specialize in management development: the Centre de Developpement du Management and the Centre des Entrepreneurs. Research is done in close cooperation with companies through the Institut de Recherche de l'Enterprise and through Chairs.

The faculty of the Groupe ESC Lyon includes 90 permanent professors, lecturers and researchers. It is a private institution, affiliated to the Lyon Chamber of Commerce and Industry.

1 How Europeans view management

Ideas about business have been dominated over the last 40 years first by the American management model and then by the Japanese. Their systems and approaches have been almost universally accepted as the best to learn and follow. The influence has been so great that European managers have often been looking at themselves through American and Japanese eyes, and have sometimes even fallen into the trap of considering themselves 'inferior' because they cannot make their companies function in the same way.

The reason European companies cannot function in the same way as US and Japanese companies is very simple: they are inherently different — they are European. Looking through most American and Japanese eyes, there is no such thing as 'Europeans' *per se*; They see only the *diversity* of Europe. That is because they are looking out from relatively homogeneous societies. In contrast, European society is an incredible jumble of cultures, languages and traditions.

But when Europeans step back from their national borders and look *through their own eyes* at how and where they fit into the world, the similarities that bind Europeans together become very clear. As a top executive at Lyonnaise des Eaux-Dumez remarked, 'There are enormous differences between a Dane and a Greek, but you only need one trip to the United States to realize they are both Europeans.'

A cartoon some years ago captured it perfectly. Three Japanese businessmen enter a room filled with Europeans clothed in every sort of national dress, and the first confides, 'These Europeans all look alike to me!'

The study on which this book is based was undertaken to discover if there is such a thing as a European management model. Faculty members from the Lyon Graduate School of Business used the same set of guidelines to interview top directors of companies belonging to the European Round Table of Industrialists, as well as other major European, US and Japanese companies operating in Europe. The study's results were summarized well by two directors at Siemens: 'Naturally, if one considers only Europe, there are differences between the countries in the way they manage a company, but viewed globally from the outside, the differences between Europe, the United States and Japan make Europe appear homogeneous.'

The similarity in viewpoints, attitudes and approaches in European business is remarkable. Diversity still exists — and probably always will. People are Italian, French, British, Swedish and so on. But at the same time they are Italian Europeans, French Europeans, British Europeans... Managers are becoming Euromanagers — considering the entire European Economic Area as their domestic market and using it as their base to compete in world markets. And many of the strategies each is devising are based on similar realities, similar conclusions about the ways companies sited in Europe, functioning under European regulations and employing Europeans have to be directed.

THE EVOLVING EUROPEAN MANAGEMENT MODEL

There is no doubt that a European management model is evolving. Its basic characteristics are:

- **managing international diversity** Europeans understand diversity, respect it and like it. Their history and trading needs have taught them how to deal with it, and most importantly how to integrate diversity without stifling it.
- **social responsibility** European companies see themselves as an integral part of society. This means they
  - act in a socially responsible way;
  - consider profits to be one of the main goals of the company but not its *raison d'être*;
  - opt for long-term thinking on strategic decisions and investments.
- **internal negotiation** In European firms negotiation takes place

not only with 'external stakeholders', but also inside the firm — with a mixture of top-down and bottom-up communication between different levels of management and employees, and between headquarters and business units.
- **an orientation towards people** Europeans believe that people are to be served by progress — not the reverse. Companies reflect this in the quality of life offered to their workers, their tolerance of individual differences, and the way they manage human resources.

Other characteristics found to be widespread across Europe but not always present were:

- **less formal management systems** Europeans tend to be sceptical of systems, so they use fewer written rules and more intuitive management.
- **product orientation** In many companies marketing and customer service are traditionally dominated by the demands of production and manufacturing, although this situation is changing.

For many of the management characteristics examined by the study, the Europeans viewed the Americans and the Japanese as two extremes and described themselves as being somewhere in between. If the responses were divided by country, one could try to plot the different nationalities as points on a scale between the US and Japan. Stereotypically the British would be positioned close to the US end and the Scandinavians and Germans close to Japan. In reality, however, the various Europeans are far closer to each other than to either end of the scale. Moreover, for each of the different management issues, no country is always in the same position on the scale. Their beliefs and practices vary.

Are the British different?

The similarities to the rest of Europe were particularly surprising in the British case, as everyone expected they would be a distinctive island, especially after 13 years of Thatcherism. 'When you say Europeans, do you mean those who are not English?' asked one British company chairman.

Nearly every director interviewed found some characteristic

where Britain would have to be described separately, or as closer in practice to the United States than to the rest of Europe. But the conversations with the British CEOs and directors themselves did not reveal that, nor did an analysis of British thinking and practices across all the issues studied. Nor did anyone doubt that *culturally* Britain fits and belongs in the European family.

Statements by British government officials on European Community issues often sound as if the Channel is impassable and no one knows how to take a plane or a ferry, or even swim. Yet as this book shows, the cement that binds the Europeans together and makes them so similar, despite their in-built diversity, is their shared history and culture — and this is impervious to Channel water.

The business leaders of Europe — especially those in Britain — have acknowledged this shared culture for a long time. The younger generation of Europeans has no doubts about it. And a healthy proportion of the British public feels it too. It's a question of time and of emotions catching up with reason, André Leysen of Agfa-Gevaert pointed out perceptively. 'You must allow time for people to accept new things. Ripe fruit falls with just a little movement, but too early and you have to pull, and afterwards it is too late. It's the same thing with the peoples' acceptance of change in Europe. We have to accept that in some areas we may have to go more slowly.'

THE CHALLENGE OF CHANGE

No other area of the industrialized world is undergoing as much or such profound change as business people in Europe are facing today. It seems that everything is changing. Not only must managers deal with the constant change demanded by technological developments and fierce competition in global markets, but they must adapt to momentous political and social developments occurring across their continent.

Until mid-1992, western Europe seemed set on a course of convergence, with the European Community's Single Market expanding quickly to include the entire European Economic Area, and then more slowly the countries of eastern Europe.

The timetable and structure of that convergence are now in doubt. While the entire world attaches great importance to the developments in eastern Europe, Europeans feel most responsible for helping those countries transform themselves into democratic market economies, and know that they will be most affected by the shockwaves if such transformations fail.

The economic recession which Europe has suffered over the past four years is putting enormous stress on all its social systems and presenting formidable challenges for business. Moreover, it is denying government and business the extra resources they require to finance the special economic, political and social mechanisms needed to help change be harmonious at this important turning point in Europe's history.

'We are living through a phase of painful transformation,' said François Cornélis, CEO of Petrofina. 'The more I reflect on these questions, the more I am certain that the solution lays neither in withdrawal into ourselves, nor in nostalgia for the way things were in the past. I am not at all minimizing the suffering inflicted by the current phase of transition. Yet I am convinced that the fact that we are entering a new world — which is no longer one of overcautious security and complacency — is not a synonym of catastrophe. We are all learning to live with the constraints of the uncertainties of risks, the lucidity of our doubts, and the effort of constantly requestioning ourselves.'

SOCIAL CHANGE

Business must also deal with deep and important changes which are taking place across European society. The declining birth rate has produced a demographic picture indicating that in the year 2000 15 per cent of western Europe's population will be aged 65 and over; by the year 2020 that figure will have climbed to nearly 20 per cent.

The role of women is changing across Europe. In all countries increasing numbers of women of all ages are moving into jobs in the public and private sectors. This is partly the result of women receiving more equal education with men over the past 20 years, families deciding they need or want two salaries, and employers recognizing the valuable human resources that women represent.

Family life continues to be extremely important to Europeans, but the traditional family structure is being turned on its head. In many countries, young couples no longer feel the need to marry, even after they have children together. Young women no longer believe they can or should expect to depend on a man to supply their lifelong financial needs. Responsibilities in every area of life are being shared more equally between men and women.

People below the age of 40 do not have the same attitudes to work as their parents and grandparents. They want jobs that are satisfying to them as individuals, goals to which they can feel personally committed, opportunities to develop themselves in a well-rounded fashion. But at the same time they insist on balance in their lives: they cannot be 'owned' by a boss and they put limits on how much time they will trade for money. Men as well as women value their personal life and want to have time and energy to invest in it.

THE RESPONSE TO CHANGE

The developments we have described are having a profound effect on European society. Both business and government will have to respond to them. This book shows that the business leaders of Europe are alert to all these changes. Among the seemingly chaotic economic, political, and social forces at work, they recognize many strongly positive elements. The challenge for business is to grasp these positive forces and direct them towards the convergence and regeneration of the European economy.

The members of the European Round Table believe this can be done. Moreover, they are convinced that European managers have the capacity to grasp the opportunities of Europe's new Single Market and use it as a base to compete successfully in world markets. In this book the ERT members and other directors talk about the steps their companies are taking in this period of renaissance, the characteristics European managers share, and the lessons they believe Euromanagers need to take on board.

'This subject of European management is very important,' reflected José-Alberto Blanco Losada of Telefónica. 'Europe is moving towards the recuperation of leadership. In a certain fashion, one can see it and recognize it. Europe is in the process of regaining the world position it has held so many times before. And it isn't happening in a temporary or makeshift way. This leadership which I see coming is a consequence of our way of viewing the world. And if it is this view which has enabled us to survive all the barbarians, all the metamorphoses, and even the European civil wars ... well, there must be something of value in it, eh?'

2 A changing order

The interviews given by the European business leaders in the survey are reminiscent of the Renaissance in the 14th to 16th centuries, when the commercial class imported new ideas with its goods and opened every level of society to enormous change. The conversations lasted one to two hours and were conducted in French or English — often the directors' second or third languages. The thoughts expressed were deep and philosophic. The directors spoke of a more open society, greater development of the individual, exposure to foreign views and ideas, the need for continuous learning — similar values to those espoused in Renaissance times.

The business leaders interviewed have a very realistic understanding of the difficulties, complexities and implications of Europe's present situation. There is also a clear recognition that it is up to business people to take the lead; the economy will have to be strong enough to provide the means for the political and social developments to mature, for the continent to move forward in harmony. But with that solid realism comes positivism, a nearly tangible sense of what it is possible for Europe to achieve.

There is no precedent for the unification of European countries which is now taking place, said Pirelli's Jacopo Vittorelli. 'When Europe was unified before — by Rome, Charlemagne, and so on — there was no industry and companies did not exist. So everything we are living through on that level is totally new.

'We shall live a new experience, creating communities of companies, with multi-languages, multi-traditions, multi-this, multi-that — it is something which has never occurred anywhere else. Twenty, 30, or 50 years from now European companies will be multi-national in the basic sense of the term — with a base in Stockholm, another in Italy, another in England.'

Américo Amorim of Portugal agreed. 'The European market is going to change in a brutal fashion. Over the next ten years, to survive in Europe — with the turbulence caused by Eastern Europe, the penetration of merchandise from all the continents, the machinations and adjustments of the Single Market — it will be imperative to have a global vision.

'European directors moved in that direction fairly timidly to about 1990. But now they will do it far more deeply. It's an imperative because the turbulence is a sign of the start of a new world economic order.'

A NEW WORLD ORDER

The perception that we are entering 'a new world order' leads to caution and risk assessment, but not fear. Europeans have survived a myriad of turning points in their history. Theodore Papalexopoulos of Titan Cement voiced this precisely: 'We must be proud of ourselves and not only of our ancestors.'

In the view of Helmut Maucher, Chairman and CEO of Nestlé, 'the centre of Europe has moved more towards the East, so it includes eastern Europe now. I sense the end of this great period of Anglo-Saxon domination of management methods which we have just been through. I think we're going to see a new mixture of cultures, of traditions, of thinking. And certainly, automatically with that will come a little of the philosophy of the East, influences from the Slav and a little more from the Germanic — in a good sense.

'In my opinion that is also going to change a little the "management style" in Europe. For instance, one of the most important things will be this idea of "*Gemeinschaft ist mehr als die Wahrnehmung gemeinsamer Interessen,*" the community is more than just the defence of common interest. There's a spiritual dimension to this idea.

'The "management style" and the way people work in Europe is going to take into account certain ideas from the Japanese, hold onto a certain Anglo-Saxon spirit of the free market, and combine them with many other influences. But it will also have to take into account the culture, the value of Europe, the individualism of the people of Europe, which is different to that in the United States, because it is a commitment to certain values, certain ways of life developed in the humanist tradition. In Europe "management style" has to mobilize this individualism, this "self-value" for the profit of the company, but without killing the value of the individual.

'This is a question that is very important. These days the values of the people show a little more hedonism than in the past. Sometimes it seems that they have an attitude of optimizing their private life, of using society as a tool to gain money. And there I think, with good management, with "employee involvement" and such, one can again reach a better balance between the "commitments" for the company and optimizing the quality of private life. It's a question of giving priority to balance. Of course one can run a company without motivating and mobilizing the people, letting them continue to just work with no tie, no commitment to the company. But how much better to manage it so that employees keep their individualism, their human values, their self-respect and, at the same time, enrich themselves because their work and the company add something interesting to their lives.

'Europe can reach this kind of balance because we can mix the modern desire for options with the values from our past, our traditions. We are in the process of changing, but we have to be the right kinds of managers.

'The management of people in business has gone through a period where it was too narrow. There was a great deal of talk about "professional managers" — of engineers, technocrats, marketing, etc, and that's not sufficient any more. For me, it is far more important that managers have a general education. By that I don't mean that they have to be able to hum Beethoven's Fifth Symphony. But that they need a true, wider understanding of our situation: of the people of today, their values, the way they are developing, of politics, the economy, developing technologies, to be able to put their work into the context of this evolution. That to me is the real education needed — not an ability to list all the tributaries of the Mississippi.'

THE IMPORTANCE OF BALANCE

Robert Horton, formerly of British Petroleum, voiced very similar views. 'There is also one other aspect which is very important. That is that every person is given an opportunity to get outside of their work environment for a significant amount of time, periodically in their career, because the tendency to social normalization — to think that the way in which we do something is the only way in which it can be done — is enormous.'

Horton spoke from personal experience, having accepted the chairmanship of BP after managing companies in Europe and the United States. He explained a thesis held by Professor Ed Schein of the Massachusetts Institute of Technology, which puts forward the idea that any strong culture develops its own set of rules, norms, and regulations, 'and if you stay, are retained within that culture and not rejected by it, it is because you accept those rules and regulations. And that can become unhealthy.

'You can induce independence of the mind by taking people out of the organization and sending them to a business school, or saying "take three months' sabbatical, go and write a novel, or go and read philosophy if you want, or whatever else interests you, so that you refresh your mind and can look into the organization from the outside."

'It's very important that we all understand that our life with our business is only half of our life. We have got to have a balanced life. The BP vision statement declares it in print: "We encourage our employees to strike a balance between their responsibilities to BP and to their home life."'

'You have a balanced life?' the interviewer asked the oil mogul, somewhat incredulously. 'I have a balanced life. Yes,' replied Horton. 'I have a family, I collect books, I listen to music, and I enjoy sport.'

MAINTAINING BALANCE IN TURBULENCE

So European directors see a new world order on the horizon. To take advantage of the changes and seize their positive elements, business needs the right kinds of managers. Understanding developments in technology will no longer be sufficient. Managers will also need to understand political, economic and social developments in order to put their work and what is happening to their companies into the wider evolving context.

To keep their equilibrium when surrounded by turbulence, managers will need to have a capacity for criticism and self-questioning, and an inner sense of balance. The theme of balance was repeated again and again in the interviews. It is one of the key elements in the European view of life.

3
The European view of the world

The 'American dream' and 'Japan Inc' are phrases that summarize a large set of concepts, beliefs and feelings that form part of American and Japanese societies, and describe the way those people look at life and behave. It is hard to think of a similar phrase which could be used for any of the countries of Europe.

Yet we know that the citizens of each country carry with them a common set of concepts which have been developed and tested over time. Beyond that, Europeans across the continent seem to share a way of looking at the landscape of life. We can call it the 'European view of the world'. Again and again in the interviews, these shared perspectives came through the words and ideas expressed by the European business leaders.

'Business in the United States is concerned with quantities, numbers, and performance far more than with people,' commented Theodore Papalexopoulos of Titan Cement. 'In Europe, it seems to me, one insists more that humans are, and should be, at the centre of our thought and philosophy.'

ECHOES OF HUMANISM

Papalexopoulos and many others voiced echoes of humanism, the intellectual development that marked Europe's transition from the Middle Ages to modern times. Europeans have an inherent interest in the quality of life — at all levels of society. No matter how greatly they admire science and modern technology, Europeans believe people are to be served by progress — not the reverse.

Optimism

Europeans' optimism is anchored in an inordinate sense of reality: they learn from their history that disaster can come round any corner. To illustrate 'vision' in a course on management, a European professor of business studies uses a cartoon of two caterpillars looking at a butterfly. The caption reads, 'Now *that's* a vision!' He explains, 'One caterpillar says to the other, "You see, if we are not eaten by a bird, that's what we will become!"' Most Americans would see only the vision.

Shrewdness

Europeans have great admiration for Americans, but also think they are naïve — perhaps because Americans give the impression that they believe everything they say. The nuances of words and the messages and ambiguities that can be delivered through different tones, pauses, and silences are part of the sophisticated weaponry that the Europeans have added to their arsenals over the centuries.

In the mid-17th century the French mathematician and philosopher Pascal wrote that there are two types of intelligence: *esprit de géométrie* — seeing things which can be proved, and *esprit de finesse* — sensing things intuitively which can only be proved later. If Europeans are forced to choose between the two, they pick the latter, believing it is better to be shrewd, cunning and clever than simply rational.

The realistic shrewdness of Europeans stops just short of cynicism, a word which derives from the Greek word *kunos*, meaning dog. European folklore teaches that a dog will never voluntarily poison or kill itself. A dog will obey and perhaps even love its master, but *in extremis* a dog will seek its own survival. History has taught Europeans about survival. Whereas in America people often had to fight against the elements, in Europe people struggled mostly against their fellow men.

Security

Europeans also draw on a sense of security handed down through their history: the rise and fall of Greece and Rome, the age of discovery, the colonial empires, the great wars . . . Europe has been through better and worse and survived. If our ancestors came through, so can we.

Europeans used to believe that wars could solve problems. In the 20th century they realized how fragile their civilization could be. Technology has been developed to such an extent that war must be avoided — at least on their territory. (The Balkans are a dreadful exception. They are considered an aberration by other Europeans. At the start of the present crisis in the former Yugoslavia, as European Community diplomats walked from meeting to meeting shaking their heads in appalled disbelief, their Dutch leader would intone, 'Remember, this is the Balkans.') One wonders to what extent this change in attitude towards war is due to the increasing participation and influence of women in European societies and the coming to power of the Sixties generation. Once again there are strong echoes from Europe's past, dating back to the women of Aristophanes' play *Lysistrata*. What was the Greek chorus chanting — 'Make love, not war'?

CONTRADICTIONS

There are many contradictions in the European view of the world. Although one still sees fresh traces of the class system and hears mental bows and scrapes at the mention of an aristocratic name, 40 per cent of Europeans are socialists and another 35 to 40 per cent are Christian Democrats with a strong liberal tradition. European society has been schooled and dominated by Christianity for nearly 2000 years. While Christianity in all its diverse forms failed to persuade most Europeans to turn the other cheek, it did leave indelible marks. Along with a firm grasp of reality, a readiness to deal with disaster and a guarded sense of optimism, Europeans favour a social market economy, and have a sense of responsibility and paternalism to those who work within their sphere of influence, and a belief that people are important.

Such contradictions are part of normal life, in the view of André Leysen of Agfa-Gevaert. 'We often have the temptation to be extremely rational — but the world isn't rational. Even in business the rational doesn't always work. Emotions play a big role, and it's those who know how to work on the emotions who obtain many things which you cannot reach with Cartesian logic, because humans are not Cartesian.'

'In Spain, the heart has always been more important than the head,' commented José Alberto Blanco Losada of Telefónica. 'But when it comes to business, at the point of negotiating, for example, a Spaniard is much harder than an American. In fact, it often surprises them!'

Reflecting on how to describe European management culture, Blanco Losada sighed loudly and said, 'There's a Spanish writer and thinker who you may know, named Antonio Gala, and he said, "Culture is the fashion with which one regards life and awaits death."

'And that captures it, doesn't it? We expect differences between the Japanese and the Europeans, but if we make the comparison to the North Americans, we also see great and clear differences. The culture of the United States is one of professionalism. European culture has always been more humanist, leaning far more to the generalist, much more committed to a good general level of education.

'The US economic system is extraordinarily competitive, and that probably allows companies to be far more rigid concerning norms and to occupy themselves less with personal aspects of their employees. It's even reflected in the American films. There's one I saw where a group of long-time friends are in business together, but at a certain moment a problem arises in the firm, and all of a sudden it's "I don't know you, it's your problem." And that's the end of it.

'That is not at all the style in Europe. In this company, for example, all systems of discipline are extremely hidden, masked. Care is taken in the treatment of all the personnel, and we try "not to spill any blood" as we say here.'

Pehr Gyllenhammar, formerly Executive Chairman of Volvo, reached similar conclusions. Europeans and Americans look at the people in their organizations very differently, he said, in terms of respect for individuals, trust, confidence. 'I think the United States traditionally can be very brutal. I don't think Europe is always good, but it is less brutal. However, the trends seem to be converging.'

The current economic crisis is putting European directors' humanist values and sense of social responsibility to a severe test. 1993 was supposed to mark the beginning of a brave new market in Europe, filled with opportunities for business and employment. Instead, company directors are struggling to retain their workforces and dole queues are lengthening. The contradictions in the European view need to be reconciled in a new way.

'Our certainties are shattered,' said François Cornélis pensively. 'And the famous European model which we formerly defended — often with conviction, sometimes with arrogance — is being challenged. We are questioning it. We are living through a moment of European history which is out of the ordinary, exceptional.'

THE DESIRE TO SURVIVE

European history gives contradictory signals: while it generates feelings of continuity and security, it also warns that disaster can come round any corner. As a result Europeans are notable for their desire to survive, their affinity for self-preservation. This can be both an advantage and a handicap. For example, Europeans are less likely to be the first to put forward a new idea, risking everything on a new project which might have a marvellous future. They tend instead to hedge their bets, and would probably prefer to back several projects in a number of fields at the same time. This can be judged as a quality or a fault, but either way it has an important influence on the methods, management and culture of a company.

Managers are also more prudent because of their sense of responsibility to employees and the social stigma attached to firing people. Their attitude does not encourage them to say, 'This is an interesting project, I'm going to jump into it and recruit some people. If it doesn't work, well I'll lose money but I'll fold it down and start another project.' All of these characteristics have links with the spirit of entrepreneurship.

And this points to yet another common characteristic of European management: the notion of simply making money is not the fundamental base of a company. Even though profit is the aim of each business, it is not the only reason for the company's existence. The long-term survival of the company is often considered just as important.

A SUMMARIZING VIEW

Roland Berra, the Head of Corporate Executive Resources at

Hoffmann-La Roche, reflected at length on the question of whether there is in fact a European management style. He arrived at his conclusions after comparing practices in Hoffmann's companies in Europe, the United States and Japan, as well as drawing on his own experience in Asia, Africa and Europe, working for American and European companies. In many ways his views summarized the beliefs of all the European directors interviewed. 'Social context and past history have a very great influence in Europe, just as they do in the United States and Japan,' Berra said. 'Despite the differences between European nationalities, there are many ties that bind them.

'One thing that is very fundamental,' he said, 'is the strong sense of social responsibility we have in Europe in nearly every country. Another is the need for independence, autonomy, and a constant questioning of authority. In that sense, too, our company is very European. Everything that looks centralized or regulated seems autocratic and is looked upon with suspicion.

'This cultural aspect is in fact well accepted and the company operates with much fewer corporate rules than any US company would do. The differences can be observed within the group. While an American moving to Europe will find European management less structured, less disciplined, more chaotic, a European starting work in our US operations is surprised to find that there is a set of responses for practically every question: it has been reflected upon and regulated.'

Berra related Europeans' constant questioning of authority to another common characteristic. 'The humanistic approach of the Europeans, which places more emphasis on people — with all their weaknesses, explains the lack of illusions about leadership. "Who is ever in charge?" is a question posed by Pierre Casse, a professor at the International Institute for Management Development. "Are governments in charge? Are CEOs really in charge?" That way of teaching leadership leaves much more room for individual responsibility than looking for heroes with the vision and power to solve all problems.

'The American idea of "performance appraisal" gives another indication of the differences in management style and basic attitudes,' said Berra. 'In the United States such appraisals are considered absolutely essential. In Europe, it's thought that something like this should take place, but far less formalized, much less structured. It comes about from a much more constant contact, a dialogue between the boss and the employee, and they discuss the matter together. In Japan, on the other hand, the concept of appraisal is absolutely not accepted by the companies. The bosses refuse to discuss personnel matters with their subordinates. This is not something which fits in the Japanese culture. There one evaluates a group.

'All of these differences in culture between the Americans, the Japanese, and the Europeans mount up,' Berra concluded, 'and form a very great influence on managers and the way in which they direct business.'

A CULTURAL HERITAGE

The 'European view of the world' is not as compact or succinct as the 'American dream' or 'Japan Inc', but it exists all the same, combining shared characteristics, perspectives and beliefs:

- an almost cynical realism schooled by history;
- a belief that individuals should be at the centre of life;
- a sense of social responsibility;
- a mistrust of authority;
- a feeling that all people have weaknesses and sometimes one has to 'muddle through' life;
- a desire for security and continuity;
- a belief that maximum profit is not the primary aim of business.

This package of characteristics is part of every European's cultural heritage.

4 Managing International Diversity

One of the characteristics that binds Europeans together so closely is their ability to handle diversity — their awareness of it, their ease with it, their tolerance of it, their understanding of it, and above all their capacity to integrate it. Again and again one sees the European character dealing with the complex, the contradictory, the ambiguous, and somehow creating order out of it. One can paint a mental picture of a Euromanager sitting at a desk juggling differentials and integrals at the same time.

To carry the mathematical imagery a bit further, we can compare the Japanese, American and European approaches to diversity with three simultaneous equations:

- Japan = lack of diversity
- United States = homogenization of diversity
- Europe = integration of diversity.

Japanese society's lack of diversity is almost universally acknowledged. Robert Horton's opinion was that, 'Japan is the ultimate homogeneous society.' In the United States, where immigrants have sought and received refuge since the country's inception, society is a more complex combination. Nevertheless for both personal and national reasons, the vast pot-pourri of immigrant cultures has been voluntarily blended and meshed into a culture instantly recognizable as 'American'. Even Japanese born in the United States look and sound more American than anything else! The only ones who stand out distinctly from the society are the native American Indians, who preserve their own culture on their reservations.

So it is not surprising that the American and Japanese management models being taught in business schools around the globe are based on cultural homogeneity, and view diversity as a problem — something to be overcome. Europeans regard things differently. As Baron Daniel Janssen, Chairman of Solvay's Executive Committee, pointed out, 'We in Europe have a world vision, but we believe that the world is heterogeneous. We respond better to heterogeneity because we live it every day in Europe.'

'This is our métier, especially when you come from a small country,' said fellow Belgian André Leysen. 'We always keep ourselves open and have the habit of seeing the others' point of view because we know we depend on the others. The trait tends to go in inverse proportion to the size of the country. But now even Germany and France have had to develop it.'

Leysen, whose family is so European that it has no one common language, gave an example of how European diversity works on a daily basis. 'When a Frenchman receives a letter and he is not in agreement, he does not respond. And that sends the message "I do not agree." On the other hand, when a German writes a letter to you and you do not respond, you are sending the signal, "I agree." These are things you have to know!'

THE PROS AND CONS OF DIVERSITY

From the start Europeans learn that cultural diversity is a natural part of life: this is the way the world is. Dealing with diversity and integrating it is one of their unusual strengths. Once Euromanagers view diversity in this way, they can teach their companies to use these special skills in the best way. And they can also teach them when it is appropriate to stop differentiating and start taking a global approach.

'Reconciling integration and differentiation between the countries and the activities they are responsible for — well, if I had to find a statement which was the *raison d'être* for my corporation, this would be it,' said Brian Goldthorp, Director of Personnel at Trafalgar House. 'We are now operating with 50 main-line companies in 50 countries, in all the continents of the world except the Antarctic. And I believe that what we are about is recognizing the differences, trying to bring together the parts that can be brought together and, frankly, accepting that there are limits to what we can do as corporate managers, ie the idea that we could possibly globalize and make everybody accept things in an undifferentiated way.

'I believe this integration of diversity is a very European concept. I mean, it would be quite impossible to work in western Europe if you were not capable of doing this. It is the only way we can manage our markets at the moment. As a consequence, it makes European corporations enormously strong in the parts of the world where there is a lot of differentiation and where pulling parts together in an integrated way is a difficult and complex issue.

'But the reverse side of that coin is that when we look at parts of the world where these pressures of diversity are not as overwhelming as they are in Europe, we continue to concentrate on dealing with differentiation, so Europeans are less successful there. American and Japanese corporations show the reciprocal traits. They are enormously good where there are products and strategies of an undifferentiated kind.

'For example, they can market soap and certain kinds of consumer products very successfully all over the world because there are not problems of differentiation of a major kind. You are not putting unlike parts together in an integrative process. But when it comes to dealing with the complexities of other kinds of business markets, they are less successful. What we Europeans clearly need to do is to use those strengths of integrating diversity where and when appropriate, but have a focus that is global in the less differentiated areas.'

Integration and differentiation

Pehr Gyllenhammar of Volvo also feels that responding to diversity is not always a strength. 'Sometimes it is a mercy not to know too much. Very well informed people and very bright people sometimes get confused. Decisions for them become complicated. For those who know less, decisions become simpler. It is amazing how sometimes people who have a very primitive sense of something still succeed.

'I've seen examples where companies who really do not know a market still succeed in it. They do things the same everywhere. But there are also those who set out to market only one global product with a great determination. Look at McDonald's hamburgers. There are many examples of products that are standardized for the world and that go everywhere. I don't think that a Sony Walkman looks different in Brazil than it does in France. And I think in automobiles the days are gone when you needed a different design for the south than the north. People are becoming more used to globally traded products, although there are still exceptions. It depends on the product.

'So I agree that this sense of history and respect for differences in cultures is very strong in European management. And I think it is good to understand how to differentiate. But we must also recognize that there are exceptions to the rules, where simplistic approaches work.'

Jean-Louis Beffa, Chairman and CEO of Saint-Gobain, agreed. 'You cannot let the differentiation turn into a kind of paralysis. European groups have to be ready to stop differentiation when it becomes a national specificity that no longer has justification. That's why today in Saint-Gobain we are putting more of an accent on integration than on differentiation.'

André Leysen sees other pros and cons. 'The advantage of diversity is creativity, in my opinion. The handicap is that it is sometimes accompanied by a kind of mental protectionism in people, and you need a certain period of time for adaptation before the different systems harmonize.

'I'll give you a very simple example. The company Agfa-Gevaert was merged in 1964. After that there was an internal stalemate. Three years later the company was facing disaster because no one was able to take decisions and move. They called me in as chairman, not because I know anything about chemistry, of which I know nothing, but because I can work with the Germans and the Flemish.

'The merger had been made 50/50 — two nationalities, Belgian and German, 50/50. And what did we find? The German direction would say "yes", the Belgian would say "no". And so it went: "if you do this, I'll do that." It was a classic case, just like in Belgium. When Flanders builds a port, the Belgian government gives 100 kilometres of highway to Wallonia so that everybody will be happy. But it's not rational. So finally, after 15 years, we decided to fuse mentally. We changed.

'I had seen quite early on that we had to change the structure of the company, but knew that we had to wait for the right moment, because Gevaert is not only a Belgian company, but a Flemish company — the first great Flemish company. Selling its shares is a bit like selling the Arc de Triomphe in Paris.

'Finally a crisis arrived: the price of silver skyrocketed. We consume 2.5 tonnes of silver every workday, so we needed to augment our capital. The Belgian side didn't have it available, so we exchanged titles with Bayer, the "mother" of our German side. We gave 100 per cent of our stock to Bayer and became shareholders of the German group. All of a sudden the mental barriers fell. The Germans and the Belgians began accepting things because they no longer had the feeling that they had to defend themselves.'

WHO HAS THE KNOW-HOW?

'Europeans have the know-how for managing diversity,' commented José-Alberto Blanco Losada of Telefónica. 'We can all play with it. The problem is that we do not all know how to do it to the same standard.

'There are some British companies who have been sending their staff abroad for 50 years already who are perfectly adjusted to the situation. We at Telefónica are relatively new at this. That's why we started out in Latin America, where we have far more affinity with the language and culture. And it's not by chance, I believe, that we also have a presence in Romania — the only Latin country in eastern Europe.'

As Wisse Dekker, former Chairman of Philips, pointed out, because many European firms started out in relatively small home markets, if they wanted to expand they had to do so by going to other countries. This historical fact plus their almost inbred acceptance of diversity has enabled Europeans to develop the ability to work successfully in other cultures and countries and to use the national human resources they find there.

'European business is possibly more open to the world than the United States or Japan,' reflected Ernest Van Mourik Broekman, Group Director of Human Resources and Organization at Shell. 'Of course, the Japanese are vitally dependent on exports, but their understanding of the way that other countries operate their industry, of other countries' styles, and their willingness to immerse themselves in other countries has only recently become evident.

'As far as the United States is concerned, their home market is so vast that companies often feel no real necessity to adapt to foreign markets. Moreover, when US business goes abroad, it tends to control those operations in a very centralizing fashion. It is very much control from the home front. We are much more decentralized in the way we operate and the levels of authority we give our operating companies than our US colleagues in the oil business.

'My experience shows that it is reasonable to say that European business leaders are better equipped to deal with cultural and geographical diversity than most American managers, but that would not necessarily hold for the Japanese,' said Willem J. Guitink, Philips' Director of Management Training and Development. 'For instance, look at Canon Europe. They used to have 450 Japanese managers running the business in Europe. They came from Japan for four, five, or six years and they learned to deal with diversity.'

However, Guitink added that when large numbers of those managers began returning to Japan because their assignments expired or for their children's education for example, Canon was faced with a situation where it had to hire European managers to replace them. Canon did not find this easy, as it meant having to imbue the Europeans with Japanese culture so they could work effectively with the company's headquarters in Japan. 'Having to include European managers in their Japanese culture Canon found more problematic than having Japanese managers running their businesses in Europe.'

Global vs local

'I'm always very worried when I see too many non-locals in companies,' said Floris Maljers, President of Unilever. 'We have a very international management. I think if you have a strong group of local people, you are at least in contact with the local culture. If you add to that a small number of non-local expatriates at a senior level, then they can contribute if there is ever an international issue. So what we like to get, for example, is French management with a French approach in France, but with a few expatriates who take care that it doesn't become so French that it is no longer internationally part of the Unilever group.'

Hoffmann-La Roche also believes that having national managers is an advantage. However, in order to develop a more global company culture, explained Roland Berra, 'the company encourages key people to gain experience in other countries. So the Italian manager, having worked for some years in the United States, will look at the business world differently than if he had stayed all his life in Italy.

'Purely national thinking can also be a detriment for an international corporation because a decision taken in Paris, for example, might have repercussions in other parts of the world. A company which operates globally needs managers who think globally even when they are posted in their own country.'

Japanese homogeneity

Many of the directors interviewed pointed to Japanese firms managed only by Japanese as another proof of a cultural need for homogeneity. Dominique Turcq, a Japanese expert from McKinsey's Euro-Center, writes in his book, *L'inévitable partenaire japonais*, about how Japanese firms have great difficulties dealing with multinational culture. Hiroshi Kosaka, who works within the Group Executive of Toshiba in Tokyo, makes similar points.[*]

Wisse Dekker expounded on the matter. 'Let's look at how European companies integrate diversity. When a European company invests in another country — such as the United States or Japan or South America or another European country — we are not afraid of transferring technologies. We also like to establish laboratories for research and make use of the other talents we find there. Philips, for example, has been very active in east Asia and especially in countries like Taiwan. We have an outward view and the Japanese certainly do not. They are totally different and give as little as possible.

'They want to have an assembly factory only if it is necessary and if they cannot export their already-made products. If it is not necessary, they do not go any further. Gradually they are understanding that they have to go further, but it is happening little by little. In our philosophy, on the other hand, it is necessary to make use of French talent or British or German or whatever to make the whole company

---

[*] See Turcq, Dominique, *L'inévitable partenaire japonais*, Librairie Arthème Fayard, Paris, 1992, and Kosaka, Hiroshi, 'International Competitive Strategy: a Japanese Perspective', *Gestion 2000*, No.3, Université Catholique de Louvain, Louvain-la-Neuve, Belgium, June 1993.

stronger. The Japanese are afraid that if they give power or control away, they will lose it. We are not like that.'

Decentralization

'We try to decentralize,' said Sir Antony Pilkington, the fifth generation in his family to run the glass manufacturing company which bears their name. 'We let our subsidiaries run their operations in their own countries and we control them by financial means. There are few British nationals operating in our overseas operations.

'For example, we started our Swedish company on a greenfield site — nothing there except a pond and some duck — and we built a big industrial plant. We had about five or six English people over there at the start, but now it's entirely run by Swedes.'

Hoffmann-La Roche also leans towards decentralization in many areas, explained Roland Berra. He believes their policy is linked to the acceptance of different cultures. 'The desire to be at the leading edge of science — a position we maintain — has led the company to have research in a number of countries: the United States, England, Japan, Switzerland. It also led to the acquisition of a majority shareholding in Genentech of the United States, which is one of the most advanced companies in biotechnology.

'The company tends to develop businesses where the human talents are available,' he said. This has led Hoffmann-La Roche to create centres of excellence, 'not in the Head Office alone, but where the know-how is. For example, a unit based in Montpellier in France is responsible worldwide for the haematology activities of the Roche Diagnostic Division.'

UNDERSTANDING AND RESPECTING OTHER CULTURES

'The Japanese and Americans try to explain away our different approach to working in world markets by saying we are simply more used to historical and cultural diversity than they are, but it goes deeper than that,' mused Marc Fornacciari, Director of Planning for Lyonnaise des Eaux-Dumez.

Blanco Losada threw some light on this with a personal anecdote. 'I think the Americans, for the most part, do not comprehend the concept of diversity. Because the Americans not only do not adapt to other ways, but they export their own culture and try to implant their own "American way of life".

'This story will explain what I mean. Telefónica, you know, is part of a consortium with a contract to privatize the telecommunications industry in the southern half of Argentina. Okay, at one point we were in competition on a tender with Bell South of the United States. And do you know what they did? As their representative to Argentina, Bell South sent a black woman who could not speak Spanish.

'I could not believe it. She was an excellent professional, there wasn't the least doubt of that. But to a country like Argentina — which is a white, male-dominated country with a culture totally rooted in Spanish Europe — they send a black woman who speaks no Spanish. They failed from the start! What a mentality! Who took the decision to send that person there? To me it reveals a total ignorance of the contexts in which one has to move and work.'

Walter Schusser and Hans-Jörg Hörger of Siemens have had similar experiences. 'Siemens is a good example of a European company,' they said. 'It has always felt that it must become part of the country where it establishes itself, and work in accordance with that country's laws and customs. In other words, in France we want to be seen as a French company, in Brazil as a Brazilian company, etc. So we were really stunned when a US company in Germany declared, "Here we run on American policies, why should we have anything to do with German laws? There's no question of setting up a Workers Council; we are an American Group!"'

Paul Roettig, Senior Vice President of Austrian Industries, who works closely with the countries of eastern Europe, explained a similar point with a more serious story. 'I worked in other countries for a good part of my life. I worked for 18 years for Exxon in Austria and in the UK, for a long time in Africa, in the United States, and so on. And in the Ivory Coast one day a young man (I remember his name was Bertrand) asked me, "What right do you have to transform us into the western model? You want us to learn American accounting methods and American methods of direction of human resources. Okay, I agree. But what right have you to change our fashion of thinking, to try to change our philosophy?"

'I think that is what we must often ask ourselves — and even more often ask our managers. What right have we today truly to transform people in their way of being, in their culture, in their manner of seeing life?'

No imperialism

Jean Pierre Doumenc and Didier Guibert of Groupe Schneider agreed with Roettig. 'In the end, despite our colonial backgrounds, today we in Europe are less imperialistic. The Americans and the Japanese like to export their total model: business, culture, methods, tools, everything. Whereas we have this very deep intercultural regard. Look at the way the Schneider Group succeeded with Federal Pacific in Canada or Square D in the United States, which was our big acquisition in 1991. We let Square D continue totally as it was in terms of company culture. We did not intervene at all. Maybe Europeans do that because our cultures are more mature, and we know what it's like to be confronted. We have a long tradition of dealing with a multicultural environment.'

Trafalgar House, said Brian Goldthorp, has exactly the same policy as Siemens. 'Although our subsidiary companies are part of our group, we want them to develop as national companies in each of their settings. We make sure that we operate them as companies that are specially careful to fit the rules and the culture of the country in which they live.'

They also require top management to have a very strong national team, with nationals represented in many of the top jobs. This is very different to the approach taken by the Americans and the Japanese, Goldthorp explained. 'Both try to reproduce their own corporate culture in the country to which they are going, but they do it in different ways.

'I think typically the American imposition tends to be of a forceful and rather unsubtle kind. It tends to be a combination of three things: first of all, "hard-headed" business executives are imported from the United States to run these companies. Second, policy documents, handbooks, company laws are brought in wholesale and they are defined as being the operating practice in the company. Thirdly, there is an enormous bureaucratization in these companies through detailed American accounting reports that must come in monthly.

'Characteristically, the Japanese operate somewhat differently. They bring over a top manager who is Japanese, who has very close links with the parent company back in Japan. They bring in local nationals to be a part of the management team. These people are expected, in fact, to take on a Japanese style of working and a Japanese approach. The manager and his local team take extensive steps to try to change the attitudes of the people working in the company — managers, supervisors, and operatives — to accept, and *want* to accept, a Japanese style of working. So theirs is a more persuasive approach, to show the benefits of the Japanese style, while the American style is more, "This is the way we do business; this is the way to operate. Take it or leave it."

'Our approach is diametrically opposed to that, and I believe ours is a European characteristic. It is a difference between what is essentially an autocratic, imposed style of doing things and one which is a more cooperative stance. I believe our method is not only culturally, ethically and legally a sound practice, but also that it is better for business.'

Company culture

André Breukels explained the way in which Hewlett-Packard runs its international organization: 'We have a culture within the company which I would say overrides the local culture. So if you walk into the Hewlett-Packard offices in Oslo or in Madrid, you would pick up the similarity of the Hewlett-Packard culture much faster than you would recognize you were in Norway or Spain. It is very interesting. Communication between people, open office design and style, a very informal way of behaviour . . . . Even in Germany, where one would expect to find a very hierarchical style of behaviour, if you walk into our factory in Stuttgart you will find the same Hewlett-Packard cultural style as in our other offices.'

'There is a very great difference between the Europeans, the Americans, and the Japanese on this point at the moment,' commented Hiroshi Wakabayashi, General Manager for Business Development for Itochu Europe.'The flexibility of European directors permits them to reduce the difficulties that exist when running operations covering many Continental countries at once.

'Most European managers speak English, French, and German and know the news and what is happening in each European country. The fact that the social, cultural, and historic contexts of the countries are relatively similar help the Europeans to learn quickly. And they need to. It's a necessity of the market. It seems hard for foreigners to catch up to them. But in my opinion, the Japanese will develop themselves in the same manner after sufficient time and experience in Europe.'

A 'GLOCAL' APPROACH TO THE SINGLE MARKET

Ralph Cooper, President of Coca-Cola's European Community Group, agreed that the Europeans excel at diversity. 'Successful European managers uniquely deal with a more complex business environment than either the Japanese or the Americans, in my view. They have to deal in multiple cultures and multiple currencies and multiple regulations and multiple governments, and a whole host of things.

'But when you are dealing with cultural differences, I think it is important to understand whether it is business-to-business or business-to-consumer. There are different approaches, different styles, and one has to be able to accept and do business within the confines of the culture. For example, if you go to Brussels to do business with a Belgian company, you are not going to have a 30 minute lunch. Languages are very important. But I think the business discussions may well be the same.

'In Coca-Cola we're seeing a dichotomy taking place in business today. Some of the customers of the Coca-Cola system in Europe, such as large international companies, are becoming more European. Many of them want one programme for Europe.

'On the other hand, the consumer is becoming more local, in our view. We are advertising Coca-Cola in Barcelona today in two languages — Spanish and Catalan. It is a recent phenomenon and we see it taking place in Scotland, Wales, the French regions, the German Länder . . . . People are becoming more culturally attuned with their localities and marketers have to recognize it and be prepared to deal with it.'

To deal with the new Single Market, Ralph Cooper explained, Coca-Cola is trying to combine a 'European concept' with local implementation. He runs the European Community Group from Atlanta, Georgia, with a staff of five plus the functional heads of finance, external affairs, marketing, etc. 'But my operations are in Europe, where we have a European Operating Board that I meet with in Europe once a quarter, and sometimes more often, to discuss strategies, aims, review operations, and share experiences. So we are much more integrated than ever, but the marketing is still very local, underneath an umbrella strategy.

'Let me give you an example. In supply, I have a person who is head of supply for Europe. Why is that? Because we looked at our infrastructure. Take a simple case like cans. If we let each country manage its own can business exclusively, somebody somewhere is going to run out of cans because all of a sudden the weather is very hot in Germany, or in France, and the business takes off and that operation runs out of cans. In the past we would have lost those sales because we were operating inside that country. Now we have a European supply group whose job it is to make sure that we always have an ample supply of finished products — whether it is coming from franchised bottlers or from company-owned canning facilities or wherever.

'1992 was a prime example. We had the UK business struggling a little bit in the early part of the year. Then all of a sudden there were changes in the activities: a little warm weather in May and the UK operation was on the verge of being out of stock. In came the supply group. They went around Europe, sourced some cans, and sent a million cases to the UK. Ten years ago there would have been a big scramble and probably we would have lost half a million cases. Today we lose nothing. It's the European concept with local implementation.'

Integration

Robert Horton also structured BP in a spirit of integration. 'When I took over I inherited an organization that was designed to have 12 businesses in 70 countries. But when you looked at it, we really had three businesses and three regions: America, Europe and the Far East. Once you make that sort of intellectual breakthrough, you can do all sorts of things. We saw that we didn't have to have separate brands in the United States, Europe, and Japan, so we rebranded the whole thing.

'We now run the corporation worldwide from London, but the refining and marketing company for Europe is sited in Brussels, so we run the UK from Brussels. It was a hell of a fight because people said, "you can't do that" and kept devising more reasons for that. But of course the savings are enormous. Instead of having 12 head offices, 12 research centres, 12 sales forces, you have one of each. And instead of having 12 strategies, you have one.

'I do believe that you should segment markets, but by product. You should not segment markets simply by geography. And I also believe that it is immensely important that you understand the diversity and culture of each country. So I ask that all my managers speak another language and that they immerse themselves in the culture of the country they are working in. Even though English is becoming the international business language, I believe it is important for our managers to speak the language of the country because you understand people through their language.'

'When one speaks one language, one is in a world of one dimension,' said Theodore Papalexopoulos of Titan Cement. 'When one speaks two languages, one is in a world of two dimensions. When one speaks three languages, one is in a world of three dimensions. With each language it is like opening a door onto something completely new. And this dimension gives you the possibility not only of understanding the words, but of functioning like the other person facing you, who comes from a different world — even if that person comes from a world of only one dimension. And the more languages one learns, the easier they are to learn.'

There are many lessons which European managers can learn to help them take advantage of their natural skills as their companies move across the Single Market and into the rest of the world. As they proceed, François Cornélis, CEO of Petrofina, pointed out that 'Euromanagers should try to bear in mind that even companies have national personal traits. Our companies are what they are partly due to the country from which they first drew their origin and strength. For one it could be the system of Les Grandes Ecoles, for another the demands of the consumer, for yet another the quality and specificity of their nation's universities.'

Adapting to diversity

'There is no doubt that the diversity of Europe raises some problems,' said Gavino Manca, Pirelli's General Manager of Economic Affairs.

'It is more difficult to manage a European business than one in the United States or Japan. The fragmentation of Europe is not only a cause of difficulties, sometimes it is also a waste of time.'

'But it also helps develop managers' abilities,' added Pirelli Vice-President Jacopo Vittorelli. 'Because if you have to adapt to the diversity you have to become more capable of dealing with it compared to the Americans and Japanese, who never have to deal with it in their own country.'

'Yes', agreed Manca, 'but we can be sure this scenario of European unification will reduce the fragmentation and differentiation in Europe and that managers will be pushed to integrate their businesses.'

'Some differentiation will be eliminated, some reduced, but a lot will remain,' insisted Vittorelli. 'So the job in the Single Market will be to do both — integrate and differentiate at the same time.'

'It can be done,' said Papalexopoulos of Titan Cement. 'I picture it in my mind like the human body: it is a unity, yet at the same time it has all these different parts able to move in different directions doing different things. As an ensemble they form the individual, who is unique.'

INTEGRATING DIVERSITY

To succeed in the Single Market, companies will have to be able to integrate diversity. Many companies are recognizing this by building the integration of diversity into their operating structures for the new European Economic Area. What results is a European form of the 'glocal' strategy and organization, mixing global and local approaches.

Euromanagers have a competitive advantage in this area because they come from such heterogeneous backgrounds: to them, diversity is a normal part of life. By comparison, Americans and Japanese come from homogeneous cultures, so they tend in general either to minimize diversity or to view it as a major problem.

The propensity to integrate diversity can turn into a disadvantage, however, when it is taken too far. As US and Japanese companies have proved, with some products it is smarter to be simple, ignore the differences and 'go global'. The challenge for Euromanagers is to recognize when to play their diversity card and when to hold it back.

One of the key questions for the next 10 years is whether European firms will demonstrate superior skills in reaching a 'glocal' balance. They probably will be able to do this on the European scene, which they know best. The answer is more uncertain for world markets, where some American and Japanese companies already seem to be balancing their purely global views with more and more local responsiveness.

5
Social responsibility

European managers see profit as one of the basic aims of a company, but not its *raison d'être*. Profit is a means to a larger end.

There was near unanimity among the ERT directors on this point. Everyone described US companies as almost totally directed towards the bottom line, where the shareholder, not the customer, is truly the king. Everyone described Japanese companies as involved in an intricately woven social spider's web that connects them with the state, government, trade unions and employees, so that they function in consensus as 'Japan Inc.' The Europeans placed themselves between those two points, in a type of social market economy, and when discussing their philosophies and practices revealed themselves to be closer to the Japanese than to the Americans.

European directors see their companies as always needing to act within a social as well as an economic context, because they believe their companies are 'owned' not just by the shareholders, but also by all the people involved with them: employees, clients, suppliers, creditors, local communities, etc. They acknowledge that all these stakeholders have legitimate interests in the future of the company, and this influences decision making and planning. As a result, European directors tend to take a much longer-term view than their American counterparts, who are seen as being tied to quarterly results. But the Europeans still feel bound to take the interests of their shareholders into account and to produce revenue for them. Their thinking is consequently less long-term than the Japanese, who are seen to be free to act over a much longer time frame because of the interlocking alliances which provide their capital structure.

A BROADER PURPOSE

Hoffmann-La Roche decided to review its corporate principles in 1986, after the Chairman had restructured the company. 'We formed teams to ask ourselves what we wanted to fight for, what was our purpose, our *raison d'être*,' said Roland Berra. 'Naturally, we had different currents of opinion. There was the more American school which thought that we ought to state that the primary purpose of the company was to make money.

'Another school of thought was more science-based and said, "We have a long tradition of research, of knowledge, of relationships with the medical profession. Thus the aim of the company is above all to make progress in science and to achieve solutions to health problems. Profits should be the results of this progress, not the primary purpose.

'Others felt that the company had a moral obligation to the public at large: the patients needing better drugs and services, the environmental concerns, the employees, and the communities depending on our activities.

'Ultimately — and this is quite typical of the European cultural environment — it was felt that if the company was not able to meet and combine all these *raisons d'être*, it would be missing something. Only the sharing of many deeply seated values would be worth the full commitment of everyone.'

This viewpoint resembles that of the Japanese. Hiroshi Kosaka of Toshiba described it as follows: 'In Japan, even though many of the institutions and practices of western capitalism have been adopted, the pursuit of profit is not perceived as the final goal. The final goal is the welfare of the people, and profits and capital formation are only tools employed, usually unconsciously, to this end . . . It is therefore unconsciously perceived that the true owner of the group or company is the employees and not the stockholders. Because the employees view themselves as the company's owners, the sale of the company, which provides for their daily needs, is unthinkable.'[*]

---

[*] Kosaka, H, 'International competitive strategy: a Japanese perspective', *Gestion 2000*, No 3, Université Catholique de Louvain, Louvain-la-Neuve, Belgium, June 1993.

Yet there are still strong distinctions between the Japanese and the Europeans.

THE COMPANY AS PART OF SOCIETY

'Social performance is not a direct aim for us,' explained Didier Guibert of Groupe Schneider. 'European directors believe a company has social responsibilities and, even wider, a type of citizenship role to play. But this occurs as a side-effect.

'While maximum profit for the shareholders is not our sole aim, I think European companies have become more and more conscious of economic performance. More importantly, I think that they have completely integrated the fact that they can only attain economic performance by taking into account very strongly their social responsibilities — both internal and external.'

The British view

Nearly everyone interviewed expected the British attitude to these issues to be far closer to US corporate thought than their own, because of the influence of Thatcherism, the City, continuous Conservative government rule since 1979, and the Major Government's insistence on keeping apart from many aspects of European Community social policy. Yet the British directors interviewed showed that this was not the case. They align themselves with the other Europeans when talking about social responsibility, but among the Europeans, the British are the closest to the Americans.

The viewpoint of Robert Horton, former Chairman of BP and before that CEO of Standard Oil in the United States, was almost identical to that expressed by Didier Guibert. Horton was very clear about the aims of BP and designed its vision statement himself. It is shaped like a target with shareholders at the centre, but their benefits have to be attained via the surrounding quarters of equal opportunities and challenging careers for employees, mutually beneficial relationships with suppliers, customer satisfaction, and exemplary standards of community ethics.

'I believe that maximum shareholder value is the fundamental end,' Horton said, 'but I also believe that you will not achieve it unless you have due regard for the other stakeholders. I think the mistake many companies made in the 1980s was to say that you drive the company simply by looking at that single objective. I don't think you can.'

Sir Antony Pilkington took a very similar view. 'We have been a public company for 20 years, and were a private company before that. We don't consider and never have considered that the maximum profit for shareholders is the fundamental aim of the company. That comes as the product of success; it is not the starting point. We have always taken our social responsibilities seriously and we believe in the balance between employees, customers, and community — even countries for that matter.

'I would not say that social performance is just as important as economic performance, but it is an important factor. We are not something separate — just a body of people founded by some shareholders operating on their behalf. We are part of the structure of the town we work in and the lives of the people we employ and of the country in which we live, and I think it's ridiculous to pretend otherwise.'

Interdependence

'Maximum profit for shareholders cannot be the essential aim of a company,' said Walter Schusser of Siemens, 'because maximum profit today is not necessarily maximum profit for tomorrow. That depends on investments. To manage a company professionally, you always have to look at the results in terms of durable security, the long term.

'For us, economic performance and motivation are the base of a company's capacity to perform socially, and the three are tied together. The bigger a company is, the more social responsibility it has. In that sense, pressure groups like unions are perfectly legitimate. The public interest has to be respected. Suppose that Siemens wanted to lay off 5 per cent of its employees in Germany. That represents 5 per cent of 200,000 — or 10,000 people, an enormous number. If we were speaking about 5 per cent of a company of 200 people, there wouldn't be much fuss. But 10,000 redundancies would be in all the newspapers. We should not forget that a company does not work in a vacuum. It profits from an economic, governmental and social system, and thus it must respect a certain interdependence with the system.'

Pehr Gyllenhammar of Volvo believes that previously, when European companies thought more on a national than an international plane, economic and social priorities were more evenly mixed. 'It is a mark of European companies that social performance and being a good citizen is important, but I think economic performance has now taken priority. There is an understanding that without good financial performance you will not fulfil your other responsibilities.'

THE PRICE OF A SOCIAL ROLE

Brian Goldthorp of Trafalgar House thinks that European companies pay a price for their social role. 'It has desirable characteristics, but in certain circumstances it may mean that the firm is not as successful in obtaining its market share, developing its products, etc, as against the competition from the United States and Japan.'

Roland Berra offered an interesting example. 'In our corporate culture, nearly everyone feels a double responsibility — to the corporation which has to get results, but also to the people, with their strengths and weaknesses. So often decisions will be based on a mixture of economic and human aspects.

'In purely economic terms, management could be much more demanding. But there is a great deal of empathy for people, even if their best is not optimal. This attitude on the part of management creates a high degree of loyalty and dedication towards the company, which is not unlike that found in Japanese organizations.'

In Japan there is a great deal of social pressure for dedication to be a two-way street: loyalty to the company is expected to be rewarded by lifelong employment. If a company in Japan restructured and fired large numbers of employees, there would be a public outcry. In the United States, however, a large company can fire many thousands of people at a time and relatively few brickbats are thrown. It is considered part of the unfortunate ups and downs of business life.

In Europe, noted Roland Berra, 'Opinion surveys show that dismissing people for economic reasons only is culturally not acceptable, even among senior managers.'

Jacopo Vittorelli of Pirelli agreed emphatically. 'If you have to close a plant in Italy, in France, in Spain, or in Germany, you have to discuss the possibility with the State, the local communities, with the trade unions ... Everybody feels entitled to intervene — even the Church!'

Sometimes the price of the social role becomes too high, and there are massive lay-offs as has been the case in the current economic recession. This appears to contradict the orientation towards people which we described as a characteristic of the European management model. However, there are still important differences between the Americans and the Europeans in this area. One difference is that lay-offs are a last resort for the Europeans; another is the way in which such lay-offs are implemented.

As Bertrand Collomb, CEO of Lafarge Coppée, commented: 'I know that in Spain a few years ago there were companies that took the attitude, "I have a factory that is doing nothing, but I have 150 men there, so I won't close it." That was also the attitude taken by French companies 30 years ago, but no longer. Faced with that situation today, I would close my factory — but I would try to do it in the most humane, intelligent way possible. If I thought there would only be a "black hole" for six months, I wouldn't close the plant. In the same circumstances an American would probably close the factory and perhaps reopen it a year later.'

LINKS WITH GOVERNMENT

Brian Goldthorp of Trafalgar House drew on personal experience to explain the differences he and others saw between the American, European and Japanese attitudes to the 'social market economy'. 'In the United States, where I have worked extensively, I think there is very much more the characteristic that we in the corporation are alone, unto ourselves, and indeed, might be a more important pressure group than the State, the Federal government, or certainly smaller and less important pressure groups like trade unions.

'Frequently in the United States you can see companies spend a lot of time outflanking the requirements. Even if the Federal government puts pressure on, it is not considered to be part of the corporate ethos necessarily to obey rules or take them seriously into account if you can find methods of defeating them without a penalty.

'In the United States I see no evidence of institutionalized linkings and communication between the state, local authorities, trade unions, pressure groups, and companies to regulate a social market. I think the parties are really quite distant and only occasionally seek co-operation for tactical reasons. In Europe, the players are clearly differentiated from one another, but are always involved in dialogue about this "social market economy".

'In Japan, where I engaged in an exchange as a manager within a Japanese company, things take place on a more subtle level. Somewhere at the boundary the state, the government, the corporation, the trade unions are all the same. Somewhere all these organizations merge together, and they are really one basically. It seems to me that very often they don't need to discuss the requirements of the social market because there is the consensus that all their actions are predicated on that anyway.'

Hans Merkle of Bosch went a bit further. 'I am persuaded that the European entrepreneur feels an obligation to the whole ensemble of society, but not in a nationalistic sense. Whereas for the Japanese, success for the company is also success for Japan.'

Government involvement through industrial policy is another area that differentiates management in Europe from the United States and Japan. François Cornélis of Petrofina pointed out that, 'In the United States there is a bigger separation between business and government, despite the lobbying power of corporations and the activity of legislators at various levels of government. The commercial game is very hard, very direct, very cruel.

'In Europe, the game is more subtle, if not more underhanded. The governments of the big countries have industrial policies and have developed networks of businesses that complement each other more or less, together forming a national fabric. As a result, management is more protected by the public powers than in the United States. But this, I expect, will change in the Single Market.'

European legislation

One way it is changing is through harmonization of legislation at the European level. This is also leading to a paradoxical deregulation through regulation, explained Viscount Etienne Davignon, Chairman of Société Générale de Belgique and a former EC Commissioner of Industry. 'In addition to government-business interaction at the national level, companies also have to be engaged at the European level, because if we want to suppress a great deal of bureaucracy, we have to begin by creating a single framework. Unfortunately, many people have difficulty understanding that.

'In Europe in order to deregulate, we must first regulate — we must first pass through a Community-wide regulation that replaces X number of other diverse regulations. And that's why we in Europe are not involved in the same kind of process as in the United States. In the US, on nearly every subject there is a permanent theoretical debate over whether government at any level has the right to be concerned with it. Business here considers it inescapable. Instead of getting involved in a theoretical debate about it, business seeks to exert its influence at all levels.'

For these and other reasons, government–business relations are close and direct in Europe. 'For important issues,' said Walter Schusser of Siemens, 'the Chancellor invites the heads of the most important companies to a meeting — say Siemens, Daimler-Benz, Thyssen, Hoechst, BASF — along with the presidents of the employers and industrial associations, and the heads of the more important labour unions. And there they have a round-table discussion of the most important issues and sort out the problems that require concerted action.'

'This kind of thing really surprises Americans,' commented one senior executive, 'but it happens here all the time'. It is fairly common in all the countries of Europe that company chairmen and CEOs will breakfast, lunch, or dine with a Government Minister to discuss an issue.

LONG-TERM THINKING

The way European managers take decisions is therefore greatly influenced by their belief that their companies are part of the life and landscape of the community, that profit is not the *raison d'être* of the enterprise, and that shareholders are one of several groups vitally interested in the firm.

If a company is 'owned' by all the people involved with it, the interests and reactions of these stakeholders must be borne in mind in the planning process. This leads European managers to use a fairly long time-frame for decision making. As André Leysen remarked, 'The Americans have a horizon of three months because of their quarterly financial reports. The Europeans have a vision over three years. And the Japanese look ahead 30 years.'

Neither extreme really tempted the European directors interviewed. For a company to be able to plan a generation ahead, like the Japanese, with no fear of reprisals if bets on investments failed, was seen as an incredible luxury, but unrealistic in the European sphere. One hears far more about Japanese successes than Japanese failures, of which there are many. 'In reality,' noted Marc Fornacciari of Lyonnaise des Eaux-Dumez, 'the Japanese companies are not that profitable, because their growth is geared to market shares, and not at all geared to return on the capital invested in them.'

'In the United States, the pressure of the quarterly corporate report has become one of the great weaknesses of their economy,' said Leysen. 'Company directors always have to prove to their shareholders that things are going better. They are judged like politicians, only worse, because elections are held every three months. If they have two bad quarters in a row, the shareholders start complaining and looking around for another director.

'It works well enough for the financial sector in the United States, at least since the 1980s, because finance can live within such a short short-term view. But industry requires investment with a larger and longer vision, and that, to me, is one big reason why American industry in general is in such distress.'

Because Japanese companies do not face the same kind of pressure for short-term profits that shareholders impose on American and European companies, they are able to develop strategies with a much longer time-frame and to operate more flexibly in the short term, according to Hiroshi Kosaka. However, in his opinion the time-span addressed by the long-term strategies of Japanese companies is no longer than those addressed by the best managed US and European companies.

American companies manifest an odd mixture of long-term strategy with short-term analyses and actions. Paul Roettig of Austrian Industries explained it this way: 'Americans reflect a long time about when, how, and where they should invest. It's not planning, but strategic reflection. They verify everything. Above all, they want to be able to state precisely if there will be profits in the second quarter of the second year. The Europeans spend much less time on strategic reflection. Many companies have a tendency to say, "The investment is agreed. We'll take the risk. Let's go."'

Royal Dutch Shell usually judges its investment decisions against very long time horizons, but this practice may be related to the fundamental nature of the oil industry, said Ernest Van Mourik Broekman. Investments are tested against scenarios of price, political climate, trading systems, etc and so require well-developed checks and balances and strong controls.

Notwithstanding sectoral differences, however, he believes all European managers make their decisions against a background of low labour force mobility, numerous regulations extending social protection, and strong staff loyalty. 'The health of European companies is therefore defined with a different emphasis, combining financial criteria with social acceptance and employee consensus.' And this occurs despite the influence of heavy US investment in Europe and American-style management systems.

CONSTRAINTS ON BRITISH FIRMS

The time-frame for decision making is one area where British directors thought they differed significantly from the other Europeans. They felt caught in a similar 'trap' to the Americans because of the nature of their capital markets. Hiroshi Wakabayashi of Itochu Europe describes it as 'management by accounting', and is amazed by it. 'The managers directing the company accord huge importance to the balance sheet and profit-and-loss.'

In the United Kingdom, about 80 per cent of company shares are quoted on the stock market, compared to less than 50 per cent in Germany and less than 20 per cent in Italy. This affects the whole structure of accountability, according to Sir Antony Pilkington. Those on the Continent can take a longer-term strategic view of industry, research and development, and progress. 'The United Kingdom doesn't have that luxury because of the pressure for dividends from shareholders, most of whom are institutional investors with pension funds which are being managed on a completely different time-scale to the companies in which they invest.

'I think the markets in the UK and US are more of a trading nature, while those in continental Europe are more of an investing nature. I mean, junk bonds could never have started in Germany! It's just impossible to imagine. And this affects the objectives of management in the trading blocs. If short-term trading, the share price and dividends are what you are expected to produce, then you are not going to invest a billion pounds in a long-term project and tell your shareholders to wait 10 years for the result. By contrast, that's much easier to do in some continental countries and very easy to do in Japan.'

Yet when asked specifically about his own company, Sir Antony cited it as an exception. 'We are different because glass is a very capital-intensive industry. We need £70 million to build a plant; it's impossible to make one much cheaper. It takes two years to build and it runs for 10 years without stopping, so we have to take a long-term view. Our shareholders have to understand that, but they find it difficult to comprehend and put pressure on the board to react more quickly, and we have to explain why it is easy to say but difficult to achieve.'

Many British directors feel that their capital market situation traps them into shorter-term thinking, and would like to change it, but they have not yet found a way to do so without making the UK market less free and creating other problems. The situation raises interesting questions about 'ownership' and brings us back to a company's fundamental purpose.

'I think there is a whole area of discussion needed on what ownership really means,' said Sir Antony. 'The shareholders provide their money as an investment for reasons they choose. But they can get out of the company much more easily than your employees or your customers. So I think the concept of shareholders owning the company is too black and white, because they have the ability to disown it too.

'I rather like the analogy somebody told me the other day. If you put a lot of money on a horse in the 3:30 race, do you own a bit of the horse? The answer is you don't. You've simply put your money on it in the hope of making some more money. So we must not claim only the benefits of ownership, but must also consider the responsibilities and obligations of ownership.'

MAINTAINING AN EQUILIBRIUM

European companies pay a price for their social attitudes. Often they have no choice: the cost is imposed by government legislation. But in many cases, company policies have also developed from cultural attitudes shared by all the stakeholders.

In many ways, the 'social market economy' was an experiment which Europe embarked on after World War II, almost in recognition that the old order of the strict class system had been destroyed along with the infrastructure, and that to emerge from the rubble of their lives people needed a new, more equal social system as well as new buildings and roads.

Now many people are questioning whether the experiment has worked, and more particularly whether European business can afford to pay the social bills while it fights through the recession. The interviews with directors indicated that there is a shift in position taking place as companies try to keep their balance.

'The people have been nourished on promises that the society can no longer fulfil,' said François Cornélis, 'because we haven't had the courage of our ambitions and have given priority to consumption over production, and to the comfort of the status quo over the risks of change.'

'You cannot talk about profits in an absolute sense,' said Justus Mische of Hoechst. 'You have a financial, an economic balance sheet, but you also have a social balance sheet. And there should be profits on both. One must remember that profits are not only an end, but also a means — enabling the company and the society to reach other ends.'

On the whole, European directors do not regard obtaining *maximum* profits for the shareholders as a healthy course for a company to follow because it does not allow a balanced perspective or lead to long-term success. They view profit as one of several essential aims, which also include securing the survival of the company and ensuring continuing employment for their workforce. In their opinion these basic goals can best be reached by working with the various stakeholders who have a key interest in the company's future: shareholders, employees, managers, customers, creditors, suppliers, and the broader community in which the company functions.

6
Internal negotiations

The ways in which the boards of European companies are structured reflect their views of ownership, and its responsiblities and obligations. This is one of the areas where the Europeans are most fragmented, ranging from the more egalitarian structures of Scandinavia to the tightly controlled family holding companies of the south. Not only are the names of the boards different in the various languages, but their types of members, rights, powers and roles differ by country as well. Nevertheless, on the whole the Europeans are still more similar to each other than they are to the Americans or the Japanese.

Every European firm finds it necessary to negotiate with all layers of staff to get things done. This extends to the relationship between a corporate headquarters and its operating units. A simple top-down approach, relaying orders from the head office, does not work. Neither does a smooth, Japanese-style, bottom-up approach. What occurs is actually closer to a multi-sided debate, in which each constituency or unit defends its own view until they arrive at acceptance or a compromise. So the decision-reaching process moves in many directions at the same time. At some point in the process, unions and worker representatives have to be involved, but the hats they wear and the roles they play vary from country to country.

In the Scandinavian countries, the relationships between staff and management reflect the egalitarian structures of their societies. At Volvo, for example, Pehr Gyllenhammar invited employee representatives to sit on the board in 1971 — four years before it was required by Swedish national legislation — 'because I believed that they should be part of the decision-making, at the top and at the bottom and all the way through.' In Germany, national legislation passed in the 1950s and 1960s required companies of a certain size to have 'workers councils' and an *Aufsichtsrat*, where representatives of shareholders and workers sit together.

But in other countries people are still struggling against the remnants of the class system. In some the dialogue between manager and employee still carries undertones of an ideological battle dating back to Marx and the social consequences of the Industrial Revolution. 'Worker participation in top-level management, in the German style, would be opposed by most Italian companies,' said Jacopo Vittorelli of Pirelli.

LABOUR RELATIONS

Most large companies deal with national unions that represent all workers in a sector, like IG Metall in Germany, or that are marked by political ideologies, like the CGT in France. Discussions can develop into political arguments with far-reaching consequences. The situation is very different in the United States and Japan.

While in the United States there are some very large national unions, as in the automobile and textile industries, relations between management and workers are mostly centred on a factory or office, based on contracts that involve salaries and working conditions. Discussions are material rather than ideological. There is also an acceptance of the top-down approach: what the boss says goes. The company's values are those of the top management team. Once the board and CEO take a decision, it can be implemented relatively swiftly.

'It is much more difficult for me to get things done in a finite time in Europe than in America,' said Robert Horton, former chairman of BP. 'In America, if I say "We are all going that way," then if we agree, we all go that way. Americans do it. In Europe you agree, "We are going in that direction," and maybe 50 per cent will go in that direction, 25 per cent will go in another direction, and 25 per cent will go in a third direction. I often caricature the difference as being instant action versus endless debate.'

Horton thinks the difference is due to the educational systems. 'Here in Europe we are brought up with the Cartesian tradition, to debate and to come up with a rational answer. Many people find it difficult to accept a solution if they don't have 95 per cent of the elements needed to come to that conclusion.'

Japan

Decision making in Japan often takes far longer. The CEO has power, but it is used in a delicate way. Every European and American director interviewed admired the way Japanese companies appear to communicate with their workforce: giving information to staff at all levels, explaining what they are doing, and allowing for everyone's participation. Questions are raised and suggestions put forward in an effort to arrive at a consensus before decisions are reached. Every person consulted feels responsible to add value. So once a decision is taken, everyone feels they own it. Implementation is entered into willingly with what appears to be total acceptance.

'That does not happen in Italy and I do not think it happens in most parts of Europe,' said Jacopo Vittorelli. 'Workers at lower positions certainly do not participate in the strategic decision-making process. And that may be wrong.'

Comparing his company's practices with those in Japan, Gyllenhammar questioned the degree of involvement Japanese workers are actually given. 'We are a bit more political: we do it because the process is important — to all of us. At Volvo we are looking for the real thing. I mean, you can have 20 employees on your board, but if you disregard them completely, they are not on your board. When we have employees on the board, we give them the same weight, role, and respect as other directors and discuss issues with them in the same terms. We have no secrets.'

Unions in Japan are company-based and are an integral part of the group. Battles between managers and workers do not happen as they do in the United States and Europe. As Jak Kamhi, Chairman of Profilo, related: 'Our company was suffering from a serious strike in 1978 when I had to go to Japan to visit Matsushita, a firm with whom we work very closely. Every day I received faxes, and my hosts asked me what was wrong. I explained that we had a big problem in the factory because the people had stopped working. And they told me they were in the middle of a serious strike too, but had no difficulties with production. Then they took me to their factory: everyone was hard at work, but each person wore a hat with a little sign that said "This factory is on strike."

'"What does this mean?" I asked them. They explained that the workers were discontented and wanted to find a solution to their problems. They could continue with production because they were confident that while they worked everyone, including the employers' association, the *Keidanren*, would be involved in solving the problem.'

Labour relations in Europe therefore differ greatly from those in both the United States and Japan. Although the Europeans encompass a wide range of variations, one can still classify the countries into two main groups: the northern system and the Latin system.

THE NORTHERN SYSTEM

The northern system is run on the basis of codetermination and consensus. In the Scandinavian countries, Germany and the Netherlands, the system evolved naturally from the structures of those societies.

Board decisions tend to be taken unanimously, with all the difficulties ironed out before the meetings. 'One can technically vote,' said André Leysen of Agfa-Gevaert, 'but over a long period in one firm I only saw one person vote against a motion, and he quit the company soon afterwards.'

Major strategic and financial decision making is done through a dual system. One half is the Executive Committee, composed of the top executives who manage the company. The other half is the Supervisory Board, chaired by a representative of the shareholders, with half the members representing the shareholders and half representing the staff. In the Supervisory Board, votes are taken and if no majority results, the chair casts the decisive vote. But here too most issues are negotiated before the meetings begin.

Generally there is a high degree of involvement on the Supervisory Board. 'Both sides work very deeply and seriously,' explained Leysen, 'especially the staff. They have internal structures — with news going back and forth from bottom to top — and are extremely well informed about what is happening inside the company, often far better informed than the shareholders. My experience has been that the staff representatives have a very good comprehension of the company's difficulties, that they know how to defend staff interests, but that they do it in a constructive way.'

In addition to this dual system, other negotiations take place between management and workers' councils. All the directors interviewed who work within or with the northern system said that the communication, cooperation, and codetermination it requires take a great deal of time, but that the effort and time yield great dividends because once a decision is taken all the forces within the company are mobilized to implement it.

Even André Breukels, now Director of Personnel of Hewlett-Packard's American Division, praised the system of workers' councils. 'I am sure they are going to be adopted across Europe one day and will be a strong influence. We use them in a very positive sense. For example, we had a sales region headquarters in Frankfurt with about 300 people which we wanted to move to Stuttgart to make a single headquarters for Germany. We discussed the whole plan with the workers' councils. They gave agreement on it, and the implementation was far faster and smoother than the dilemma we might have faced otherwise.'

THE LATIN SYSTEM

In the Latin system, decision making is generally far more dominated by the chief executive. The CEO consults with the company's other executives and expert advisers and must persuade them to agree to a common view. Matters are then taken to the Board of Directors (Conseil d'Administration), where the CEO usually has a great deal of influence. Once board decisions are taken, they are communicated and discussed with union and staff representatives. Again at this stage time is needed for persuasion before moving to implementation.

'In France,' said Jean-Louis Beffa of Saint-Gobain, 'the dialogue with the unions complements regular information flows within the company. There is a measure of social discussion, explanation, and preaching which runs through the communication with them. We're likely to take the approach: "Here is our industrial strategy. The figures indicate why your factory is not competitive enough and this is why we need to restructure." Then we would explain in detail the reasons and argue them out. In the United States, managers are far more likely to say, "Listen, there's going to be a restructuring and this is how it's going to be done."'

'At Pirelli we try to inform people that certain important decisions have been taken and that a certain strategy is being adopted,' said Jacopo Vittorelli. 'And we take great care in doing it, but we do not succeed all the time. In fact, it seems to me that we have a problem of communication in Europe.'

Most companies in the Latin system consider unions as *necessary* evils. As José Alberto Blanco Losada of Telefónica related, 'At one moment during tense negotiations, we could have had the union's back to the wall, but there was an exquisite feeling inside all of us holding us back, and we gave them room because we feel that the union is a necessary part of the company.'

Whereas in the past meetings between managers and unions were suffused with an atmosphere of anticipated confrontation, directors say that is now changing. They describe their situation as in a state of transition. They feel they are moving towards attitudes and systems that extend communication towards cooperation and consultation. As Marc Fornacciari of Lyonnaise des Eaux-Dumez commented, 'There is a sincere feeling within all the directors and managers I meet that they want to create intelligent companies, and to do that they must first convince the people of what they are doing so that everyone participates, and each person brings his stone to construct the edifice.'

THE BRITISH VARIATION

British firms are managed by a single body, the board of directors. Labour relations in UK companies tend to be run under a variation of the Latin system which has more of a throwback to the social dialogue, pitting the owners of the means of production against the workers. In the 1960s and 1970s, unions were strong enough to wreak havoc nationwide. The balance of power between managers and workers changed under Thatcherism and as a result the unions have less force and fewer members.

It is not clear in which direction labour relations in the United Kingdom will now move. But many people believe British firms will be influenced by the changes in organizational behaviour which are taking place across Europe: an effort — in the Japanese style — to communicate with the employees, understand and learn from their perspectives, win their cooperation and forge a commitment by all involved in the company to work towards the same goals.

TOWARDS A MORE UNITED APPROACH

The important changes taking place in labour relations in European companies are recognized and affirmed by both insiders and outsiders. 'Across Europe', said Ernest Van Mourik Broekman of Shell, 'the decision from above is certainly becoming less and less acceptable, not only because of legal requirements to consult, but also because it would be hard to get the commitment of people if you didn't have a process in which the objectives of the operating company were clearly stated. At Shell we try to translate those into individual objectives so that people can understand how they fit into the whole picture, into the totality of the business. It has become part of our whole process of trying to involve people in their work.'

Ralph Cooper of Coca-Cola also sees major changes. 'When I lived in London in the 1980s, in much of Europe it was the "us versus them" adversarial relationship, with executive dining rooms and a whole host of perks that set the senior executives apart from the workers.

'Europe is now changing in my view. They are making it more of a united approach to the marketplace instead of a divided house inside the company. I think responsible business is smart to find a way to make their employees feel an integral part of the team, to replace the adversarial relationship with a partnership approach. That involves share option schemes and making workers feel they are involved in the ownership and future direction of the company. In my opinion, those companies that can make that change will be the winners in the next two or three decades. Those companies that cannot make that change will be the losers.'

7
Attitudes to human resources

Business in Europe has reached the conclusion that its competitive position over the next 20 years will depend on its people. To some extent the Japanese and Americans share this view, but their response to it is different.

In the United States, business still regards people as a primary resource which can be used and then thrown away when no longer needed, noted André Leysen. 'We in Europe consider people as an integral part of the business, a concept very similar to the Japanese. The fundamental difference between us is that the Japanese have a collective society while we have an individualistic one.'

JAPANESE ATTITUDES

There are other basic differences between Japan and Europe which affect companies' attitudes towards human resources. For example, Japan is a highly homogeneous society while Europe is highly diverse, and this affects all types of communication and direction. Japanese still seem to be content to sacrifice their personal pleasure in the present for the good of the group and a better tomorrow. Europeans have reached a point where they want quality of life today. The average Japanese works 2000 hours a year compared to a European's 1650 hours. On top of that, many companies report that workers in their Japanese units take less than half their allotted paid holiday time.

In both Europe and the United States, people identify themselves by the work they do. In Japan, they identify themselves by the corporate group for which they work, say Japanese executives. For example, in Europe and America an accountant is more likely to change the company for which he or she works than to stop being an accountant. In Japan people are more likely to change jobs than the group for which they work.

These characteristics are evident in the organization of corporate groups, noted Kageo Nakano of NTT. 'Due to European individualism, in its positive senses, all the members of a European group function well but independently. But I have the impression that they do not have the same force or dynamism as our groups. It's as if 1+1+1= 3 in Europe, but 5 in Japan.'

CONTRASTS WITH AMERICA

The contrasts between Americans and Europeans in the field of human resources are less stark. Cultural similarities, the burgeoning of US investment and business units in Europe since 1945, plus the fact that the Americans were the first to recognize and treat business as a profession, have meant that many of the personnel systems in use in European companies have been imported or copied from the United States. The Hay system of classifying functions is only one example. ('Only an American would have had the nerve to try to classify functions!' remarked François Cornélis of Petrofina.). Some people believe the United States is still consistently three to five years ahead of Europe in studying human resources and devising appropriate solutions and systems.

Yet there are important differences in character, personality and outlook between Europeans and Americans, and in the way their societies are developing. Most directors recognize the differences and believe they must be built into the way European companies manage human resources. In their view, any ideas, techniques and systems borrowed from the United States have to be adapted to the local culture in the same way as those borrowed from Japan.

Americans in general are thought to be more entrepreneurial than the average European, because they are more optimistic, more ready to try something new. If they fail, they just try something else.

Because Europeans tend to be less optimistic, they are better at accepting that people have limits to their abilities. If an employee cannot be promoted above a certain level, they will allow that person to continue with the current job and appreciate the contribution he or she makes. American firms tend to take the attitude 'up or out', preferring a constant stream of young blood moving up the promotion ladder.

Europeans tend to stay with their companies far longer and to feel more of a commitment and emotional attachment to them. Successful executives seeking to switch firms can be viewed sceptically: 'What did he do wrong?' In the United States a change of company is part of the scene and is viewed neutrally or even positively, as a sign that the person is ambitious and has self-confidence.

The difference in personal connection between company and employee shows up in a variety of ways. 'In Pirelli we have a tradition that a manager retiring maintains a certain link with the company, offering some consultative contribution,' said Vice-President Jacopo Vittorelli. 'It may not always be constructive, but we do it.' When people reach retirement age, after having worked for years for the same company with dedication and loyalty, they do not want just to disappear from one day to the next.

Similarly, European workers can react with great distress if their company is sold or merged, almost as if they had been sold in the slave trade. Walter Schusser of Siemens offered an example. 'When we bought Nixdorf we incorporated our computer activities into this affiliate, which we owned 100 per cent. However, the name was changed to SNI AG. The Siemens people involved resented it incredibly. They wanted to remain part of our "internal labour market", inside the same company, and to feel part of the same group.'

Because the Japanese identify so deeply with their corporate group, they feel even more strongly on this point than the Europeans, remarked Viscount Etienne Davignon of Société Générale de Belgique. 'If I have to explain to a Japanese that we are selling a subsidiary, he responds "How can you do such a thing?! What are people going to think?" It upsets him profoundly. And I respond, "Listen, it's very clear that the people are going to be better off with the others than with me." But for the Japanese it is still an unthinkable action.'

INDIVIDUALITY AND CONFORMITY

Both the United States and Europe are considered to be societies which champion individual rights. The US appears to be more tolerant of racial and religious differences. But Europeans are far more tolerant of individual differences and less willing to conform. These traits show up in their companies. Where Americans have strict job definitions and will hire only people who fit them, Europeans are more likely to adjust the definition to the individual hired. Even when they find a round peg for a round hole, they do not expect it to be a perfect fit. There are pros and cons to this attitude. Brian Goldthorp of Trafalgar House noted that while it frees people to be creative, it can also result in tolerating inadequacy. 'My horrible feeling is that on the whole it tends to lead us to lower standards and therefore lower corporate success.'

Despite the emphasis in American culture on individualism, and particularly on personal growth and development over the last decade, outsiders sense a strong push towards conformity. Corporate cultures in US companies tend to strive for homogeneity. It is not unusual for American employees, and particularly managers, to feel they must dress in the style of their company.

European companies have a looser concept of corporate culture, perhaps considering it more realistic to aim for a group with thousands of strong personalities who are able to work well together with pleasure. While manners and appearance are noticed, dress codes are far looser and left mostly to the individual's choice and discretion.

The reverse side of the coin is that Americans adapt more easily to working in teams. This could be a result of the way team sports are taught throughout the US educational system. In Europe, apart from the UK, schools remain focused on academic work and leave pupils to arrange their own sporting activities. It is noticeable that Americans can be pulled together from different units or companies to work on a project and will be joking with each other by lunch-time, having established the necessary rapport to get the job done. It is rare to find the same camaraderie formed as quickly within a group of Europeans — even from the same country.

MISTRUST OF AUTHORITY

The concepts of leadership and direction in Europe, and the limits that various cultures insist on putting on them, combine with Europeans' strong sense of individuality to produce a dislike of rules and regulations. Lack of respect for authority is almost a sport in some parts of Europe. Just watch the way people drive. Equally it has a definite influence on the way people have to be directed and managed. As already mentioned, the top-down approach used in America is unlikely to work well in Europe, where directors find it is more profitable to create a system allowing information and ideas to flow back and forth between bottom and top.

US companies rely far more on rule books, which are accepted and followed. In addition to reflecting the top-down approach, this may be done because employees change companies more frequently in the United States and each time need to learn new sets of 'dos and donts'. Americans also seem to have less confidence in their educational system and in the basic ability of the young people entering their firms. European managers tend to impart company customs verbally, and like to leave room for manoeuvre and for people's intuition to come into play.

Hoffmann-La Roche reckons that the Europeans' natural dislike of authority can lead to creativity if properly channelled. By refusing to take decisions which ought to be taken further down, said Roland Berra, many managers in the company force their people to decide and to learn from their own decisions. This management technique encourages downward delegation not only of tasks but also of responsibilities, he said, and increases the confidence of those at lower levels in their own ability to change things.

QUALITY OF LIFE

Quality of life is important in both the US and Europe, but it is interpreted differently. American society is more materialistic and consumer-oriented. People there are more ready to trade their time for money. Europeans want a balance between work and personal life. Money does not talk in the same way to them.

André Breukels of Hewlett-Packard described how all the units in the corporation now contribute their best company practices to be shared on a global basis, and gave examples. The Americans contributed management tools and techniques; the Japanese contributed a preoccupation with quality; the Europeans contributed flexible working hours.

'The first things one learns as a manager in Europe is that you cannot make the people happy through their wages,' commented François Cornélis of Petrofina. 'Even if you raise them by 5, 10 or 15 per cent, the contentment doesn't last. Salary is not the primary motivation. Employees want to realize something with their lives, they want to feel they achieve something with their day, they want to be able to wake up every morning feeling happy to be going to work. So the manager has to create this enthusiasm and develop an organization which allows it to be expressed. It's an enormous job — and it requires continuous attention!'

LEARNING FROM JAPAN

European companies are now seeking ways to manage human resources on a pan-European level. One of their main aims is to build a closer bond among their units — to integrate the diversity. Another is to develop new approaches to human resource management that will capture the plus-points of the European personality, enable it to grow and expand within the new conditions of the Single Market, and turn it into a force that works for the benefit of both the individual and the company.

In their search for new approaches, European companies have been turning increasingly to Japan to try to discover how managers there motivate their employees and create harmony, intense involvement and deep commitment to the company's goals.

Japan's success with W Edward Deming's Total Quality Management philosophy has persuaded many large European corporations to introduce TQM programmes, but the phenomenon is not as widespread as in the United States. Nor are the results as obvious. In service sectors and customer-contact points across America, cheerful voices ring out 'Hello, I'm John, how can I help you today,' and 'Thank you for using Company A,' and 'Have a nice day!' Workers may have been programmed at the start, but the message has filtered through to their daily behaviour.

European service staff are still being coaxed to be civil. Thus companies in Europe are reaching the conclusion that their employees cannot be trained in the same way. Individualistic Europeans can be taught that quality service is important to their company and therefore to their own future, but they don't like to sit in 'group therapy' sessions to discuss quality, or parrot set phrases at people, or wear identical uniforms to prove they belong to the group.

Teamwork is another area where the Japanese excel, and a habit European directors now believe is essential to instil in their staff. 'We are finding more and more that it is not geniuses we need for success, but competent people who know how to work together, to seek solutions together. Team solutions are almost always better than individual ones,' said Roland Berra of Hoffmann-La Roche. Other directors agreed entirely, particularly since some areas of business are becoming so specialized that each individual can only contribute a thin slice of the whole pie.

But here again, European companies are finding they must approach the goal from a different direction to the Japanese and Americans. European culture does not prepare people to work in teams. Managers usually come from an educational system geared to producing stars, who have to work in isolation and compete fiercely to show how they can shine. France's Grandes Ecoles are just one example. Many of the human resource directors interviewed spoke of how newly recruited executives with university degrees and doctorates have to be trained in basic 'people skills' before they can be useful to the company.

'We like to recruit people who have a strong personality, who are genuine, but they must be willing to integrate, cooperate and support a group,' explained Berra. 'Those traits go hand-in-hand with an ability to develop the intuitive side of oneself, to use one's instincts and senses more fully with problems instead of purely a rational approach.'

'FEMALE' CHARACTERISTICS

All these traits — plus consideration of others and service with a smile — have traditionally been used to describe women. They are characteristics that have been bred into the female sex for centuries, and developed by women's traditional roles. What better training for customer service could there be than having to figure out the needs and desires of a screaming, speechless and greatly loved infant?

As increasing numbers of European women are entering and

remaining in the workforce, European managers are discovering that women offer the qualities which the modern company needs and desires. The role of women is explored in more detail in the next chapter.

8
Women in Business

The position of women in business in Europe is about to undergo a transition from market push to market pull. In the past women were knocking on managers' doors and trying to hard-sell themselves and their ability to perform in the once male-dominated domain. Soon companies will be opening their doors and trying to entice women in. All the signals point in the same direction: economic conditions, demographic patterns, the cost to society of education and training, the rise in single parent and dual income families, greater competition, and companies' need to hire the very best recruits available.

If we took a survey of Europe's top companies today, we would probably find that fewer than 5 per cent of senior managers were female. Most of those would be in the 35 to 45 age-bracket; relatively few would be aged over 50. Women in the United States might look down their noses at these numbers, believing that they have made far greater progress in integrating themselves into corporate life. Over the past 20 years Americans certainly have achieved greater quantity. But European women in the top posts say they believe that Europe's slower, more natural evolution will prove to be more balanced and of a higher quality.

Why? Because Europe's women are holding onto their 'femaleness' while succeeding in business. With few exceptions, they retain their female characteristics and values, marry and have children while holding onto their jobs, and insist on the need to lead a balanced life. Europe's women executives very rarely consider turning 'male' just because they are entering a male domain. Instead they are behaving naturally, delivering a very high quality of work, watching their numbers increase, and waiting while the atmosphere around them slowly and inevitably changes, like the intensity of light as the sun rises.

SCANDINAVIA LEADS EUROPE

All the countries in Europe have seen a great deal of change in women's employment over the past 20 years, with the pace quickening each year. The change is not uniform, however. The Nordic countries are far ahead, with 75 to 80 per cent of women working outside the home and 5 to 10 per cent of senior positions held by women. Nor can this social change be described as smoothly seeping southwards down the map of Europe. Germany is regarded as leapfrogging ahead in legislation but behind in practice.

Scandinavia is leading Europe in this area for several reasons. Its society as a whole tends to be egalitarian. Women began working outside the home in the 1930s and have continued to do so. Most people today at all levels of the private and public sectors grew up with grandmothers and mothers who worked outside the home, so it is accepted socially. Males and females expect to have to share household and parenting tasks. Educational levels are equal, although tradition still seems to point more females towards the arts than the sciences. Middle-income families need two incomes to be comfortable. Males and females accept that they will earn equal incomes. Society provides childcare support systems and school timetables that allow parents to work.

The Nordic countries are the only ones in Europe where all these statements hold true. In France, real change did not begin until 20 years ago. 'The girls of my generation are really breaking the ground,' remarked Elisabeth Bukspan, now Director of External Affairs for Total. She entered the Hautes Etudes Commerciales — one of the Grandes Ecoles — only to find that females were siphoned off into a separate school (HEC-Jeunes Femmes) and offered salaries 30 per cent lower on graduation. 'To me that was unfair and unacceptable,' so she steered herself into the public sector, entered the Ecole Nationale d'Administration, was ranked top in her graduating class, and became France's first female inspector of finance. 'When you have a prominent job in France, there are no barriers at all — you are treated equally, and that's why I wanted to start in the public service.'

Almost all the European countries have seen women climb through the ranks initially in the public sector and the professions, where the criteria for progress are well defined. In northern Italy, for example, where it is now absolutely normal for women to work outside the family, they still find jobs and promotion easier to obtain in state-owned businesses because career steps are based on exams and seniority. Across Europe the media exposure given to competent women in the public sector made it easier for women to enter business and feel accepted within it. Women in politics, however, were usually not considered as influential, because in many countries they were there 'for show'.

ABILITY MORE THAN AMBITION

When they are hired by companies, women's rise towards the top is earned through sheer competence and quality. Every woman director interviewed said her primary concern at entry was to find a post that would allow her to put into practice what she had learned, and provide her with challenging and rewarding work. None had begun with an ambitious career plan. None feels she is competing against the people around her. Instead they are intent on reaching the highest standard of performance which they feel themselves capable of attaining. Many remarked that promotion for them was a case of being eager to do a good job, and then being in the right place at the right time. In French companies today, said Elisabeth Bukspan, once a woman is hired and proves her worth, she is respected and given equal treatment. But some noted that it is still necessary for women to be twice or even three times as good as a man to arrive at the same position.

'I think this holds true for all female managers,' remarked Regina Matthijsen, Manager of International Industrial Relations at Philips. 'We have to double-check whatever we do, whatever we produce. This is a double burden on us for the time being, but perhaps the next generation will have it easier. Men have it easier. They can take short-cuts and even if they're caught in the short-cuts, colleagues would probably excuse it and say, "God, he is so busy." But if a woman is caught taking short-cuts they say, "Well, I told you she can't really do the job."'

It would be surprising if women with top educational credentials giving this kind of quality performance did not rise towards the top. How high can they go? There are at present extremely few women at the pinnacles of the ERT companies, for a variety of reasons:

- The first is that not enough women have been in business long enough to reach the top.
- The second is that most women in business are in staff and support functions; very few are in line management directly concerned with risk taking and earning profits. Therefore as they have climbed the ladder they have been evaluated on their professional ability but not on their managerial potential. Nor have they been developed to be managers of large groups of people.
- Thirdly, most of the successful women have chosen to combine family and job, and they are not willing to put in the extra effort necessary to get to the top. For them, the rewards do not justify the sacrifice required.
- Fourthly, temperamentally the women are not that interested in power positions.
- Fifthly, in some countries — like France, Italy, the Netherlands and the UK — the males just below the top executive compete fiercely among themselves and together guard against all other entrants.

GLASS CEILINGS

Nearly all the women managers interviewed said there were visible glass ceilings in companies in their countries, but the thickness of the glass varies greatly by country. The only exception is Germany.

Monika Düssel of Hoechst and Claudia Schlossberger of Siemens were sure that no glass ceiling would prevent women in Germany from rising to the top. Both noted that by the time someone is ready to be considered for a very senior position, she is usually over 40, so no one could protest with fears about lack of orientation and dedication, or about maternity leave. As long as women stayed in their company or their profession long enough and performed well enough, promotion would depend on their ability and dedication to their job.

'In Finland, maybe there is a thin ceiling,' commented Kirsi-Marja Kuivalainen, the Nokia Group's Vice-President in charge of Human Resources, 'but there are clear examples of where it has already been broken. There is nothing that could hinder me in that way.'

Italy has a fairly thick ceiling. Said Silvia Petocchi of Pirelli, 'There will be some breaks in the corners and then it will shatter slowly.' At the moment, she said, on the whole female recruits are outshining the males in terms of sheer ability and maturity. 'So in some years we will see short lists for senior posts with four men and six women, and then probably we shall see many more women appointed. And if and when women do get to the posts, in the worst case scenario they will be just as good as the men!'

It is the confident attitude that they see among the young women entering European companies today, plus the knowledge of the quality of the work they and their female colleagues deliver, and their understanding of the younger generation's concern to lead balanced lives that have convinced Europe's top women managers that they are going to come out ahead.

Female university graduates applying to companies are given the same treatment as males in most cases, and are hired in proportion to the numbers studying those subject areas. The exceptions are research and production, both because fewer women study engineering and the sciences and because older males tend to reserve production as their domain. Young women and men are also treated equally during training and early promotion. Differences begin to appear with career planning and advancement beyond that stage.

COMBINING CAREER AND FAMILY

By the time a woman is earmarked as a potential high-flyer, she is usually in her early thirties. Male, and even some female, department heads then pose the unvoiced question: will she choose job or family? The answer nowadays is a resounding 'Both!' — just as it was for most of the women who are in top positions today.

The economic recession, poor job market, rising divorce rate and change in attitudes towards marriage combine to make many young women feel they should not depend on a man to support them financially through life. The young women entering business in Europe today fully expect to combine family and career, choose their partners with this in mind, and are prepared to take on the responsibilities it entails. Many of those who feel they are in the fast track want to hold onto the same job and return to their offices at the end of the basic maternity break (ranging from 14 weeks at 70 per cent pay in

Ireland to 15 months at 90 per cent pay in Sweden). Many others take advantage of longer unpaid parental leave offered by their firms, and take a break of one to three years. After this period, in most cases, the women are guaranteed re-entry to the firm at the same level and salary as when they left.

This works extremely well in Finland, said Kirsi-Marja Kuivalainen. The break acts simply as a postponement in the woman's career development — it has no other long-term effects. Most of the women directors in the other countries saw this as the direction in which company policies were moving. But at the moment returning women trying to combine career and family life often find they have been relegated to a relatively narrow band of middle-management posts — no matter how superbly they did their jobs before their maternity leave.

Who cares for the children?

Company policies on promoting women and women's career development decisions often stem from the amount and kind of childcare available. Germany, for example, suffers from a dearth of childcare. Because of the way school hours and school work are scheduled, if a family does not have a relative who will help care for the child, one parent usually decides to stay home. German law gives a three-year sabbatical for parental leave. Siemens offers seven years for one child and ten years for two children. Hoechst's Frankfurt headquarters has even set up a special office to help staff at all levels to combine family and job, and is offering part-time posts to serve as a bridge while children are young.

British maternity leave is far shorter, childcare facilities are sparse and poor, and unpaid but supportive parental sabbaticals are almost non-existent. Women with well-paid posts usually opt to employ a nanny, preferring to sacrifice a good part of their salary for reliable, well-trained help in the home. The less affluent feel more pressured into a three-way choice: using less expensive and less capable help in the home, or resigning from the job, or sinking into a less challenging position to salvage some energy for the home front. In such situations, everyone loses: woman, child and company. Partly as a response to such situations, a slowly increasing trend in most European countries shows men choosing to take the full parental leave while their partners continue to work full-time, or young parents dividing the leave between them.

A GENERATION SEEKING BALANCE

The generation coming into business in Europe today has attitudes hugely different to those of its predecessors. Most males and females were educated side by side; in some countries, its the first generation to experience this. Being the children of the Sixties generation, they were raised with the principle of equality of the sexes. This was reinforced by the reverberations of the Women's Liberation Movement, heavily influenced by the United States. But again, Europeans adapted it to their own culture. Where society had before defined males as possessing one circle of characteristics and females a different circular set, over the past 25 years European society has allowed the circles to converge and overlap, freeing both males and females to develop the whole range of characteristics within them.

One result is that both male and female trainee executives entering companies today are seeking balanced lives. Money and status are less of a driving force for them. Job satisfaction is being accorded a higher priority than promotion for its own sake. They want to be well-rounded people and intend to develop themselves as such. They expect and want to share in the running of their home and the raising of their children.

As Helmut Maucher of Nestlé noted, 'The young people of today have a different mentality: they are better educated, better developed, and have more of a sense of their own value — in their relations with their boss as well.' Ralph Cooper of Coca-Cola remarked on the same phenomenon: 'People coming in are not willing to sacrifice their whole lives for the sake of the company.'

The young generation's values are very similar, if not identical, to the ones held by Europe's top women managers.

'MACHO' IS OUTMODED

The increasing numbers of women in business in Europe, the values of the young executives and the breaking of barriers between male and female characteristics coincide with the new attitudes towards business organization. 'If we define what is needed in corporate cultures in today's global competitive environment,' noted Regina Matthijsen, 'we see that the "macho" type of personality is not needed any longer.'

Companies today are seeking managers who demonstrate skills which used to be considered 'softer' or more female: the abilities to communicate, listen to others, work well in a team, support others, direct through encouragement rather than fear, use intuitive as well as analytical thinking, speak many languages, and reach good compromises through positive negotiation.

The women managers interviewed believe women will be playing increasingly important roles in European companies. 'We are in a period where we need new solutions,' said Elisabeth Bukspan. 'The old recipes are a bit stale. We need a new way of viewing things.' Women bring a fresh eye to business situations and often offer a different perspective.

To compete globally, European business needs the cream of the labour pool. Most companies now recognize that women graduating from university are a valuble resource which they cannot afford to ignore. Even companies with a freeze on recruitment in the present recession are instituting ways to attract the best women, hold onto those they have trained, and ensure they return to full employment after maternity and parental leave.

Both the private and public sectors in Europe need to continue to change if they are going to profit from the full potential that women offer. Some countries — particularly France, Germany and the United Kingdom — need to provide better childcare facilities. Educators have to destroy the social hurdles which still deter females from studying the sciences or entering research and production.

Recruiting officers should carefully re-examine their psychological tests for applicants, remarked Regina Matthijsen. They should delete or rephrase those questions which are geared to 'male determination', but which are bound to elicit different responses from males and females showing their natural emotions. Similarly, managers should stop evaluating women executives as 'arrogant' when they would use the term 'self-assured' to describe a man demonstrating the same characteristics.

Significant action also needs to be taken in the area of career planning so that both men and women are offered the opportunity to take a parenting or educational sabbatical, postpone the development of their careers, and then return for full continued advancement. Such developments are now occurring, led by the most progressive thinkers.

'EQUALITY' MUST MEAN 'EQUAL'

The top women managers are sure that the natural forces at work in Europe will evolve to bring equality within the next 10 to 20 years. All those interviewed are opposed to speeding up the process through reverse discrimination, preferential treatment or quotas. They believe such measures would do more harm than good in the end — for the companies, for women individually and in general, and for the relationship between women and men. To them, equal opportunities means just that: ensuring that all barriers are down so that women and men enter and work on *equal* terms. 'I *never* would recruit someone for Nokia just because she is female,' said Kirsi-Marja Kuivalainen. 'I hire the person who has the best skills and knowledge without noticing whether they are male or female.'

AHEAD OF THE REST

The changes companies are introducing to capture the full potential of women employees are in the same mould as those needed to capture the positive aspects of Europeans' inherent individuality and their inclination to long-term company loyalty. European managers have decided that the only way to win in the current business climate is to tap the quality of their individual employees. Business leaders are already putting these convictions into practice in their companies. And this is creating a key difference in comparison with Japan and the United States which will become increasingly evident.

Japan lags far behind its major trading competitors in this area of human resource development. But it appears that 'women in business' is one sector where Japanese managers are not interested in winning the biggest market share, or even catching up.

American women executives who have nearly reached the zenith of their professions, but felt they had to abstain from family life in order to do so, often feel frustrated and bitter towards the ends of their careers because their male colleagues were not subjected to the same pressures and choices. In the past it has always been felt that Europeans had a great deal to learn from the United States about human resources. Now perhaps Americans will recognize that they can also learn from the Europeans.

9 Management with leadership

What kind of skills do you need to head a European company successfully? To be at the head of a parade of people all dressed in the same way, singing the same national anthem in different regional accents requires a certain set of skills. To head a group of individuals dressed in a wide variety of styles, singing different anthems, who when questioned deeply do not believe anyone is 'in charge' of life requires another set of skills. Do the special qualities needed to instill coherence into the group and keep the different pairs of eyes and feet heading in the same general direction fall under the heading of management or leadership or both?

The European company chairmen and directors interviewed make a firm distinction between management and leadership. Like Jérôme Monod, Chairman of Lyonnaise des Eaux-Dumez and currently of the European Round Table, most say that the CEOs of European companies tend to be leaders rather more than their counterparts in the United States and Japan. Is that because the situation demands it?

MANAGEMENT

The word 'manager' is derived from the 12th century French word *ménage* — the organization of a household. When the European directors spoke of management, this underlying sense of organization, administration and day-to-day involvement with things and people was in the background.

American managers were considered the most 'professional' — more analytical in running a business, more systematic in their approach to business. A corollary of this is that most United States companies have far more internal rules and regulations than

European ones. Japanese CEOs present a different picture, as does their way of structuring systems in their organizations.

'It seems to me,' said Floris Maljers of Unilever, that 'management culture — even assuming that we have a general idea of what it means — is something which is not very permanent. You know, the great guiding light of the mid-1980s was a book called *In Search of Excellence*, by Peters and Waterman, two prophets from McKinsey's. Some of the directors on my board asked me to read the Dutch edition, so I did. It is interesting now to look at the list of companies which were then considered excellent and at how few of them remain. The management culture which made for success in the mid-1980s apparently had an unusually high failure rate in the early 1990s.'

This scepticism about fashionable management cultures, systems and methods was demonstrated by nearly every European director. There was also near unanimous agreement on the qualities which European directors will require to lead their companies to success in the business, social, and political climate of the next decade.

'In my opinion,' said Wisse Dekker, former Chairman of Philips, 'the top manager, the president, the chief executive, should have abilities to manage as well as to lead. This is a very difficult and sensitive balance. It is also the responsibility of the top manager to be receptive, to have an appreciation of what he wants to achieve in the longer run and of conditions beyond his company which are important for it, like creation of the Single European Market. This same description may be less true in the United States and more so in Japan.'

'In Europe, the balance of stakeholder interests — those of shareholders, employees, customers, local communities — can lead to a diffused role for management,' said Ernest Van Mourik Broekman of Shell. 'These interests have to be continuously combined with immediate operational needs. There is more emphasis on managing the stakeholder networks, which is really a leadership issue.'

LEADERSHIP

'In America,' remarked Robert Horton, former chairman of BP, 'with few exceptions, I found that business leaders do not show outstanding leadership. They generally get there because they have displayed a particular professional expertise. I think there is probably more charisma among the average sample of European business leaders. This probably comes from our educational system, where we tend to have a greater sense of history and we tend to read much more. If you have been brought up to understand things deeply — how Napoleon, Wellington, Julius Caesar, Alexander the Great, Charlemagne, and the others thought and acted, that all stays in your thinking and probably influences you.

'The fact that managers in Europe, for example, need to take six months to close a plant because they have to negotiate with all the interested parties and manage all the processes, means that they have to develop many personal qualities. And I am sure it is the people who actually exhibit these qualities who get to the top at the end of the day.'

François Cornélis of Petrofina had the same viewpoint. 'The actions of the European manager are inscribed over a longer time span because he is under external constraints that force him to put in place a longer-term strategy. The American manager is more of a "hands-on" technician, close to business and very attached to numbers; his bible is composed of the statistics of production, sales, and market shares. The European manager believes less in numbers and is always somewhat sceptical of them. He tries to tackle his function with a higher social responsibility and a more expansive cultural background.

'The European CEO of today also spends nearly half of his time communicating: expressing the aims of the company, the means and methods of reaching them, the tactics, the strategy, the vision. And he must make the staff understand them. People cannot participate in an effort if they don't understand all the elements.'

Loyalty

'When a CEO arrives in a US company,' said Bertrand Collomb, CEO of Lafarge-Coppée, 'he imposes his strategies, his objectives, his teams, and it is often done brutally, far more so than it would ever be done in France. It's clear the Americans will respect his authority, but at the same time I sense they have a kind of anti-authority reaction towards their CEOs. They don't want to cross their boss, but they don't identify with him either. They always guard a sense of free will and want to keep their ability to quit tomorrow morning and work for a competitor. There is always this idea of a contract. He is the boss and I obey him because he is the boss, but I am not obliged to like him, or to think he is a nice guy, or to agree with what he is doing. There is far more loyalty to company leaders in Europe, and a desire for the leader to earn that sense of loyalty.'

A similar point was raised by Hans Merkle, Managing Partner of the Robert Bosch Group and former Chairman of the Supervisory and Management Boards of Robert Bosch (Germany). 'The European director is more forced to cooperate and equally is more disposed to cooperate than the American. We have learned to work *with* our employees and I think that's a good thing, as long as the ultimate decision rests in the hands of the CEO.

'Another important difference I see is that the European director feels more ties to his company than an American does. It's very rare, for example, that someone becomes a director of Shell who hasn't made his career in the company, and people who do have good chances of careers in Shell rarely quit it. This great attachment to the company is certainly a characteristic one finds in continental Europe. It is also seen in Japan, where 90 per cent of the people heading enterprises made their career in the same group.'

Moving around

'In the United States directors are passed from company to company like cigarettes,' said Américo Ferreira de Amorim, President of Amorim. 'It seems to me the role of the CEOs there must be influenced by the way they are chosen. The American society is one which lives on capital and profits. And the directors are placed by the shareholders according to changes in the structure of capital and the director's ability to generate profits.'

Walter Schusser of Siemens shares the impression that the tendency for directors in the US to move from company to company so quickly is related to the belief of many American managers that they can manage an enterprise successfully independently of its branch of activity. 'Whereas we in Europe are persuaded that one cannot succeed except where one has a great deal of knowledge about the sector, the operation, and the laws and regulations governing the field. This crowd of conglomerates which were put together during the past 10 to 20 years, and none of which have been very successful, were all part of this same charactertistic — the American belief that a good manager could direct any company successfully.'

The Siemens director also observed that in Germany the present generation of CEOs tends to be 'much more the rational manager, less exceptional from the viewpoint of charismatic personality, and much more rooted in action and systematic management.'

Entrepreneurs

André Leysen sees a big difference between being a manager of a big company and being an entrepreneur. 'I always say an entrepreneur is born; one cannot become an entrepreneur. It is a way of thinking which one either has or does not have. You can improve the quality of an entrepreneur, but if the primary ingredients are not there, you cannot make one. To me, entrepreneurs possess four essential ingredients. They know how to (1) lead people, (2) take decisions, (3) choose the right moments, and (4) choose good people. You cannot learn those principles by studying; you are born with them. Then an *exceptional* entrepreneur will also have a wide sense of culture.

'A manager is something else. That is someone with abilities which are developed by appropriate education, who works well in a structure, and who knows how to direct a company. I think you need both in a company. The entrepreneur on his own with a large degree of power in a large company is dangerous. But the other danger is that if there is no entrepreneur the company will ossify.'

JAPANESE CEOS MANAGE MORE THAN LEAD

'In Japan, the president and the executives don't have a spirit of "leadership",' said Kageo Nakano, Managing Director of NTT Europe, 'because they are not the people who created the company, they simply work for it with devotion. At the level of decision making, for example, "the top" confides and shares all his secrets and details with his subordinates (notably the heads of the departments), and then simply signs his name. Here, by contrast, the president and his executives show great involvement, initiative, and leadership. They work as much as the Japanese and sometimes even at the weekend! To me they seem very active and dynamic and I admire that very much.'

A very similar opinion was expressed by Hiroshi Wakabayashi, General Manager of Business Development at Itochu Europe. 'Japanese company directors are selected from among the best people who have been recruited and trained over a long period of time — and who have been through all the educational and social systems which prevent them from forming their own personalities. European companies, on the other hand, have a group of executives who are well trained from the start, but who are permitted to form and hold onto their own personalities. In both Europe and America importance is given to respecting the personality of the individual, so in this sense Japan differs from them both.

'In Japan, it is the task of middle managers in companies to create ideas and put in proposals to be approved by directors. That is why Japanese directors are not original thinkers in general, except for those who have created the company or who are entrepreneurs. There is a big difference between the Japanese people who are entrepreneurs and those who are directors of the big classic enterprise groups. Whereas here in Europe even the directors of the huge traditional companies have their own distinct personalities.

'However, in Europe, the directors of the big companies almost never go into the factories. They work in an office which is specially isolated for them. They try to hold onto and protect their privileges, which to me seem part of the traditional social hierarchy. This contrasts greatly with the Japanese style, where managers direct by going physically into the factory to see the situation and discuss it face-to-face with the employees.'

Fiat had a joint venture with a Japanese company and sent 60 of its blue-collar workers there to be trained. The Japanese CEO met them for dinner on their arrival and again when they left 10 weeks later. 'I was amazed,' said Umberto Agnelli, Fiat's Vice Chairman.

Roland Berra of Hoffmann-La Roche agreed with this portrait of the Japanese director. 'I've spent many years working in Asia, including Japan,' he said. 'Viewed from the exterior, it seems an extremely authoritarian and formalized management system. The Japanese are very polite to each other and very conscious of hierarchy on the surface. But the bosses are extremely close to the employees when they have to work together and find solutions to problems, far closer than American bosses.'

However, Berra sees the European picture differently to Wakabayashi. 'I believe that a Chairman and CEO have to point managers in the direction in which the company is going to evolve, give certain values, certain signals. The rest has to come from the whole company working together. Better ways of doing things ought to come from all over the company — even from the people at the very bottom of the hierarchy.'

SYSTEMS ARE NOT ENOUGH

Most of the people interviewed showed a combination of respect and scepticism for the management systems taught in US business schools. They see such systems as starting points rather than bibles, as tools which are important for managers to know how to use in the right place at the right time. They do not believe that management systems on their own are enough to run a company well. European managers also have less trust in such systems than the Americans do because the systems seem to change with fads and fashions.

José-Alberto Blanco Losada of Telefónica is a good example of the European viewpoint. 'I think that the world changes with such rapidity that the only thing one can do is have a capacity to adapt to change. You don't leave university with a book, you leave with a capacity to assimilate things, to reason, and to change. You also leave with a trunk full of knowledge which is obsolete in four years.

'Experience is important, but the world was still surprised by the petrol crisis, and by the fall of Communism in Russia. It's surprised by everything. If we were sure that the world was going to advance in a certain direction, we could try to teach about that for the next few years. But I think that is simply utopian.

'To me it seems sure that we are going to enter what is called "the fifth wave of Kondratieff" — multimedia, information technology, etc. The new modes of production will use more and more information technology, but the production process will continue to take place in a social context which grows more and more complex, and which one must direct and manage with *savoir faire* — not with techniques.

'I don't put down techniques,' he continued. 'In fact, I am very demanding in their management and use. I think it is important to be prepared for eventualities with many alternative plans. But if in the end we cannot use common sense and the capacity to change, the techniques will be useless.'

'I was inspired by American management style theory in the late 1950s and 1960s,' said Pehr Gyllenhammar of Volvo, 'because they saw management as a true function, as something that had to be developed, thought through, evolved through theory and discussions. In Europe at that time, management was more subject to tradition and intuitive flair. But both have now changed a lot.

'American management now has very disciplined, structured thinking, which in my opinion could be inhibiting. There are rule books for almost any situation. This doesn't mean that an American manager cannot develop his or her own style, but it has become so much the job of experts and consultants and business groups, that I think in some ways it has become rigid. It is probably good for those who need to learn fast, but it could be too rigid for mature individuals. In that regard, European management is more diverse, less guided by rules, less stereotyped.'

'There is a great deal of empiricism and pragmatism in European management,' observed Viscount Etienne Davignon of Société Générale de Belgique. 'If a beautiful opportunity presents itself and the reports aren't written exactly the way they should be according to the rules and regulations in the company manual, we are still going to look at it if we want to do it. But I must add that there is no important company in Europe which doesn't have procedures.

'Without them you can't evaluate what is happening. If everyone reported, amortized, treated stocks, and figured internal transfer prices in a different manner, it would be bedlam. We don't go to the detail of General Electric — we keep the procedures to a minimum. But this minimum exists everywhere, and without doubt it is larger than it used to be — and it is just as evident in Italy as in Germany.'

TOOLS AND RULES

Almost everyone interviewed said they thought that the Germans were most similar to the Americans in this area, and were probably the most formalized, systematic managers in Europe. ('The Germans have high productivity that could go even higher, but for every person working there is one making notes in a little book,' joked one director.) Everyone agreed, that is, except the Germans. And analysis of the interviews did show how this characteristic varies from company to company — rather than from country to country — within the broad limits separating Japanese, US and European firms.

Hans-Jörg Hörger, Director of Management Training at Siemens, explained: 'If we look at the formal procedures and management tools which have come to us over the years, we have always accepted those half-heartedly, knowing well that they never cover everything. The belief that everything is possible with these systems is not very widespread here.

'It is more important to accumulate experience oneself and then to use the tools. In this sense, we think our style of management is more rooted in continuity and learning from the past than in procedures. We certainly do not follow written rules to the letter. In cases of doubt, experience and common sense carry more weight than the rules.'

French companies are considered to have fewer formal procedures and systems than northern Europeans in general. But as the French say, the exceptions prove the rule. When the Saint-Gobain Pont-á-Mousson group was formed 20 years ago by his predecessor, said Jean-Louis Beffa, 'very explicit rules were fixed of how the group should function, with very formalized procedures, and the company has been following them ever since.'

BSN is perhaps more typical. 'We have a system with three levels, and everyone knows perfectly his responsibilities,' explained chairman and CEO Antoine Riboud. 'Each one knows the decisions he can take on his own, the decisions where he has to speak with the level above him, and those decisions where he must have a dialogue with executives two levels above him. In the United States, all that would be in a book. We have no books. I get the impression that in the US when the young executives are stuck in the mud, there is a book where Chapter 14, Line 7 says "How to get out of the mud..."'.

Lafarge Coppée does not find it necessary to have formal procedures, says Bertrand Collomb. 'For example, for a very long time we have not had any procedure for approval of investments, yet the company is organized and managed in a precise way. One sets objectives and has regular discussions with executives in which their work is discussed and reviewed, so this is a kind of procedure. But I would find it stupid if those meetings only dealt with objectives. This has never been written down anywhere; it's evident that when a manager has an appraisal meeting one discusses everything.'

This is a very different management style from Lafarge Coppée's Japanese business partners. 'I get the impression that they have a system which is extremely centralized and systematized. The executives they send to us have absolutely no initiative. If they negotiate something during the day here, at night they are on the phone to Tokyo giving all the details of what they said and finding out what they can say the next day. I think that's pushing communication of information to the extreme.'

BALANCING SYSTEMS AND SENSE

Brian Goldthorp of Trafalgar House thinks that companies have to find a balance between systems and creative inspiration. 'Americans are now very mechanized. That is one of the sadnesses of what has happened to American leadership. There are so many rules and procedures now that a leader can get away with not doing anything other than assuring the rules have been observed. The result of that generally is inactivity and no growth.

'European leaders often make enormous mistakes because they don't have rules and procedures that would have prevented these disasters from happening. On the other hand, they occassionally make superb effortless entrepreneurial decisions which would never have been enacted with formalized procedures. So you gain some things, but you also make more errors.

'In Japan they have rules that are followed successfully in technical development and quality standards, etc, yet none of those rules prevent them, if they so wish, from planning in the longer term to capture a new opportunity, a new market, or whatever. They seem to have the best balance for success.'

Titan Cement tries to find a balance, said Theodore Papalexopoulos. 'Manuals and rule books would be going to the extreme, and that would be a catastrophe here. But for a company to be centralized and decentralized at the same time — in other words to integrate the diversity — it is not sufficient to rely just on the spoken word.

'It seems to me a company cannot decentralize if it doesn't integrate itself with three principles: the first is to have valuable staff; the second is to have policies which are clear, known and accepted by the managers; the third is a system of control, with feedback that permits the director to see if the policies and procedures are working well.

'It's essential for the managers in the field, especially in far-off countries, to have broad framework directives that are given in writing, and not just orally. Once you have those conditions in place, you can decentralize, delegate the power, increase your field of action and improve your results. You can successfully integrate the diversity.'

LEADING AND MANAGING

One reason European managers try to cultivate a more expansive cultural background is that they tend to be judged not only on their intellectual capacities and profit-making abilities, but also on the richness of their personalities. In consequence, they pay more attention to cultural pursuits and accord them more time and value than an American manager would.

The European CEOs interviewed believe that to do their jobs properly they have to lead as well as manage. The fact that they head a far more diverse 'parade' than either US or Japanese chief executives, and are expected to play a wider social and cultural role, means they must be more visible, more vocal and have a vision of the route they want the company to take.

American managers are considered far more professional than their European and Japanese counterparts. They use systems and rules, and run their companies in a more organized fashion. Both Europeans and Japanese use a looser, more flexible environment, where company practices are conveyed verbally and room is left for managers to use their instincts and initiative.

Although European directors remain sceptical about management systems, and prefer to see new ones pass the 'fad-test' before they try them and buy them, companies in Europe have adopted many more than were used in the past. As in other areas, European directors seek to strike a balance between systems and common sense based on experience and intuition.

10 Competing worldwide

Europe's top managers identify two main challenges companies must meet to be competitive worldwide:

- putting customers and quality first;
- combining a world outlook with global strategies.

By their own admission, Europeans tend to be hampered by a fierce pride in their engineering prowess and inventiveness that sometimes overlooks market demand or even market desire. In their view, US business grows by keeping its ear on the pulse of the American consumer, while the Japanese thrive through their love of quality product design and production — providing value for money that almost does its own worldwide marketing. The Europeans believe that these are traits which they should and can learn, and that they have already begun doing so.

In terms of the second challenge, international executives are sure that European managers have a world outlook, but there is disagreement over whether even their multinational companies function with global strategies. In contrast, the same executives say, the global strategies used by Americans and Japanese usually spring from a monocultural view of the world.

By the term 'world outlook' we mean the ability to look at the world in its entirety, understanding that the broad picture is built up from a myriad of distinctive details which often interconnect in unusual ways. 'Global strategy' is defined in different ways by the companies which claim to use it, but at its base the term means approaching markets all over the world with the same product and basic marketing strategy. When executives give examples of companies which excel with global strategies they tick off Sony's Walkman, Coca-Cola, McDonald's, Nike shoes and IBM. A company can have a world outlook without having a global strategy — and vice versa.

'It's a little like the difference between saying that a company is international because it exports to other countries and saying that it is international because its strategic reflection takes into account the full dimension of the market and not simply the identity of the buyers,' remarked Viscount Etienne Davignon of Société Générale de Belgique.

Europeans' world view has been handed down since the Age of Discovery and the colonial period, when each great power in Europe had its own sphere of influence and imposed its own commercial system. Those cultural contacts are still there, providing natural markets for Europeans to investigate when they decide to step beyond their own continent's borders. Their more recent experience in their 'home base' of Europe — where they have had to deal with different languages, cultures, governmental systems, company legislation, and product regulations every time they crossed a border — tended to steer European companies into taking a more fragmented approach to world markets rather than a quasi-uniform global strategy. According to American and Japanese executives, bruises from jumping such hurdles and memories of the cosiness of their comparatively small and safe home markets also induce Europeans to seek safe niches and cooperation rather than face tough competition on the global scene.

CUSTOMERS AND QUALITY

Fierce competition in their domestic markets forces US and Japanese companies to learn how to market well and to put customers first — to respond to consumer demands and needs. The relative security domestic companies enjoy in semi-regulated European markets has made their business life easier, so they have not had to develop marketing techniques with such precision, commented José-Alberto Blanco Losada of Telefónica.

'We are also overly proud of our inventions,' said André Leysen. 'For a long time our European companies have been directed by engineers who made beautiful products and then said to the sales department: "Now go sell this". The Japanese are far better at devising products *for* the market, putting them on the market quickly and backing them with an extraordinary marketing effort. Moreover they are ready to buy patents whenever it suits them. They're not afflicted by the "not invented here" syndrome.'

Jean-Louis Beffa of Saint-Gobain agreed: 'What the Japanese do so well is to combine manufacturing with marketing, and I hope we Europeans will learn that from them. The Americans put enormous efforts into marketing, but they seem to have downgraded the importance of manufacturing.'

A story told by Siemens illustrates the differences in approach. 'The Americans have always been market-oriented, but they are willing to win their shares with simple technical short-cuts. Gearboxes, for example. In the European car industry it is habitual to manufacture gearboxes in a very clean way; all impurities are eliminated. The Americans found out that when drivers use the gearbox, impurities fall out by themselves. So they just put a magnet under the housing, and the impurities are attracted by the magnet. It works well and lasts for a long time. But a European manufacturer would never accept such a solution!'

Another result of the differences in market backgrounds, in Brian Goldthorp's view, is that European corporations tend to be defensive in character while the Americans and Japanese are more aggressive and offensive. 'For example, we do a small part of our business in the aerospace industry. When we sit down with our European colleagues to discuss some joint developments in which we all think we have a technological edge, before we begin presenting our edge to the market we want to go and speak to the regulatory agencies to make sure we are going to get a good proportion of our home business.' The same defensive mentality shows up in cars, in his opinion. 'It's a matter of "We'll keep what we have rather than try to get more."'

Furthermore Americans seem to have almost a national tradition that the customer is king and must always be assumed to be right. 'American employees seem to have it inscribed in their genes that they have to serve the client,' said François Cornélis of Petrofina. 'They understand very well that their company has to sell goods to pay their salaries. Sales are not understood in that way by European employees. They don't see it as the essential act of the enterprise.'

Customer first

It was certainly the Americans who initiated the idea of 'customer first'. The Japanese followed their lead, but adapted the methods and became skilful in marketing via another route. Instead of starting with the consumer and determining what he or she wants to buy today and tomorrow, they began with copy-cat products, then increased their quality to an extremely high degree, and backed their brands with devoted after-sales service.

Bertrand Collomb tells two stories to illustrate the huge difference between American, Japanese and European attitudes to customer service. 'Our American unit told us that we had a cement that wasn't working and that a trusted client was making some tests with it. The reaction of our laboratory was "The client is crazy. Our cement is very good. The client must be making a mistake." The reaction of the US unit was *"We* have to resolve the problem that the client is having. We certainly will *not* tell the client that he is wrong for posing the problem."

'Another time we were making some industrial plaster which we sold to ceramics manufacturers worldwide, including one Japanese company. The Japanese sent us back two deliveries, saying "We can't use this; it's making bubbles." Incredible. Nobody else had complained. All the same, we studied the problem and so did they. In time we heard from them: "We have discovered the problem. There is some copper in your plaster."

'Copper in our plaster? How could it be possible? We searched, and sure enough we discovered that one of our suppliers in a small quarry from time to time was using detonators with copper wires. Can you imagine how many grams of copper that could put into 20 tonnes of falling gypsum? Anyway, we gave instructions for the supplier to stop using copper wire detonators, and we sent another shipment to the Japanese company and everything was okay.

'*Voilà*! Six months later we hear again from our Japanese friends. "The last shipment was unsatisfactory due to copper..." We figured they were looking for pretexts to stop buying our products. But we went back to the small quarry anyway and discovered that stuck in a corner the supplier had some tonnes left over which had been mined with copper-wire detonators. Six months after our first edict, they'd decided to add a little bit of this stock to our order, thinking it would never be noticed. But our Japanese friends picked it up immediately. That shows you how quality conscious the Japanese are and what attention they pay to satisfying their customers!'

According to Wakabayashi of Itochu, European companies need to be spurred on by greater competition and far higher consumer expectations. 'In Europe, the consumers are terribly meek. For example, in a little store there can be a long queue while the sales people talk to each other. In Japan, the customers would complain at once, but here it is considered impolite to do that, so everyone waits calmly without saying a word.'

So to succeed in world markets, European directors realize that their companies will have to add to their engineering skills the habit of putting customers first and the ability at least to match the Japanese in the quality of products and services.

A WORLD OUTLOOK

United States and Japanese companies generally focus on their domestic markets first, where competition can be cut-throat. It is only when they have established themselves successfully in their home bases that they begin to look abroad.

European companies who want to expand cannot afford to do that, especially those from small countries. Their home markets simply aren't big enough. 'Just look at the three biggest companies in photography,' said André Leysen. 'Kodak sells 55 per cent of its production in the United States, Fuji sells 65 per cent on its domestic market, and Agfa-Gevaert sells 3 per cent of its production in Belgium. That's why the Single Market is so crucial to us.'

'You see the same story in the overall export figures of those countries. The US exports about 10.5 per cent of its production, Japan about 10 per cent, and Belgium nearly 70 per cent. Even Germany and France export about 25 per cent of what they produce.' The facts and reasons behind those figures have an enormous influence on the way managers view the world and the marketing strategies which they devise.

'If the Americans have a global view, it's because for them the United States is 90 per cent of the globe,' said Bertrand Collomb of Lafarge Coppée. 'If you are already selling to 250 million people, and have already reached a certain size, it's relatively easy to put aside some resources and push forward into the 10 per cent that's left and call yourself "global".'

The number of companies in the world which are truly international is really quite small, said Floris Maljers of Unilever. 'For a company to be truly international, I think it has to produce more than 30 per cent or even 50 per cent of its products outside its home base. Nestlé is a good example, or ourselves. We produce 5 per cent in Holland; even if you add our other home base, the United Kingdom, you go from 5 per cent to 17 per cent. So out of every $6 we sell, only $1 to $2 is produced in our home countries. Using that criterion Canon cameras is not an international company: it is a Japanese company which exports cameras to the rest of the world.'

The same would have to be said of a great many other companies. The major US industrial firms and the best Japanese companies have internationalized themselves very well and do take a global approach to marketing their products. Coca-Cola and the computer industry are good examples. But in general, the average American and Japanese company remains relatively provincial when compared to their European equivalents.

'I do not think the Americans have been very good at modifying their products or their services to fit easily into the countries in which they operate,' said Sir Antony Pilkington. This was a point made repeatedly by all the directors interviewed: big American companies use a global strategy, but it is not backed by a world outlook.

GLOBAL MARKETS

'There is no country in the world which has studied or written as many books on marketing as the United States,' said Floris Maljers. 'At the same time, they are the ones who seem to understand marketing the least. They understand a great deal about marketing *in the United States*, but they never analyse the differences with other countries. Instead they think "what is good for America must be good for you".

'The Japanese, on the other hand, are very aware of their homogeneous society and how different it is from the other cultures, so they make objective analyses of them and systematically find the variations. They don't rely on pre-conceived ideas like the Americans do.'

Hans-Jörg Hörger of Siemens agreed completely. 'When the Japanese decide to go to a foreign market, they acquire competence on it beforehand. For example, they send their employees to business schools in that country and then have them open offices and apply what they have learned. The Americans, on the other hand, start out with the principle that the rest of the world is like the United States.'

When both the Americans and the Japanese become enthusiastic about an idea and decide to market it globally, they act like 'steamrollers', said Brian Goldthorp of Trafalgar House. 'That is why they have dominated world markets in cars and electronics. I think European companies are less good at conceiving global strategies. Instead they are very good at finding niches. They understand this country, this block, this market-place and they tend to do very well in that.'

In discussing the way Hoffmann-La Roche conducts its worldwide operations, Roland Berra reached a similar conclusion. 'In our company there is practically no product that is not global. We launch a product for the whole world, but every country has its own timing, its own strategy. We give recommendations on the general plan and a maximum of information, but in practice it is left to each country to organize itself. So I think that leads me to say we have a world outlook in our activities, but a strategy that is less global.'

So in terms of applying global strategies, it seems Europeans are handicapped by their sophisticated world outlook that sees every country and culture as different and deserving of tailor-made treatment.

NOT EITHER/OR, BUT BOTH

The competition engendered by life in the Single Market will change the way most European companies respond to markets and customers, said Ernest Van Mourik Broekman of Shell. Like other European corporations, Shell's tradition has always been one of decentralization, while its American competitors have always taken a centralized approach, even in marketing. 'With the convergence of the European countries and opening of the markets, we are now also looking at processes for getting our positions in the various markets more aligned, driven by cost consideration and also by what customers want. You have quite a number of customers who operate Europe-wide and who require a European focus. Things are changing fast.'

Consumers across Europe have been willing to buy the same models of cars for years, said Umberto Agnelli of Fiat. It was the regulations set by each country that forced manufacturers to supply so many ranges. Under the Single Market's harmonization, the lines can be streamlined, although they will still have to produce the full range in terms of price. Agnelli believes pan-European marketing will have a noticeable effect on many consumer products, but he doubts that clothing and food will be counted among them.

Will European companies respond to a US-like Single Market with Japanese-American steamroller techniques? Or will they continue to respond to cultural diversity with differentiation?

Which tactic will prove more appropriate for world markets in the 21st century? Will the world remain a diverse place, requiring a European world outlook that allows for differentiation and seeks to integrate it only if and when necessary? Or will the country-cultures of the world become more similar as they develop, and respond better to the monolithic marketing practised by the United States and Japan? Will we one day see small screens in Chinese homes growling out the message, 'Put a tiger in your tank'?

The European directors with the most global experience are inclined to believe that companies should not take an 'either/or' approach, but rather use both — depending on their products and the markets they are targeting. Tackling Europe's Single Market will give companies the chance to use both strategies in combination before they take off for other shores. As a result, an increasing number of companies may find they are able to use their own versions of a 'glocal' strategy — offering a worldwide product line and basic marketing philosophy that are tailored to meet the needs and demands of individual markets as and when required.

11
Future Challenges

Futurology is a game very few play with confidence since the iron curtain came crashing down in 1989. Yet Euromanagers have no choice: they must try to foresee the changes and challenges of the next decade and prepare to meet them.

The directors interviewed set out seven feats which they believe European business must achieve to come out ahead in the next century:

1. Find the right interface between industry and finance.
2. Reach a balance between social protection and the need to compete worldwide.
3. Make the most of the Single Market.
4. Organize flexible companies with a built-in ability to change.
5. Seek continuous quality improvement in people as well as products and processes.
6. Apply 'customer-service' principles at every level of the business ladder.
7. Meet the problems and opportunities of eastern Europe and help the people there re-integrate into the wider European community.

Ecological concerns do not figure on the list because respecting the environment is a current 'given'. Every European director interviewed cited it spontaneously as a necessary social responsibility in which their firms are aready heavily engaged.

It is also interesting that the rapid developments in information technology and their effects on business organization were not listed by the ERT directors. This is in line with the deep historical sense that underpins Euromanagers' thinking and their general attitude to business systems. In their view, the most difficult changes to achieve are those which affect whole societies and which require concerted effort on the economic, social and political fronts. New business systems look easy by comparison: all that is needed is the money, time and willingness to institute them.

THE INDUSTRY/FINANCE INTERFACE

As Europe's industrial companies spread themselves throughout the Single Market they will be calling on capital markets and a financial sector that are also in the throes of great change and harmonization. What business leaders fear most is that during this period, Europe will be unduly influenced by the 'check-in/check-out' mentality of US financial markets.

European companies will want and need the backing of mobile international financial markets, especially as eastern Europe becomes more interesting, noted former Nokia Group President Simo Vuorilehto. So there is widespread acknowledgement that more information will have to be provided to shareholders, and more attention paid to their wishes. But for the European model to retain its values, business will have to hold out for the principles it believes are essential for success: a long-term perspective, stability, and continuity within a social market economy. Such continuity is seen as building in continual change, made possible by working with employees who are committed to the company's goals and have joined in creating them.

The picture painted looks similar to the Japanese approach, yet it differs in the important details of quality of life and profitability. 'We have to remember,' said Bertrand Collomb, 'that the Japanese used their steamroller strategy during a period when they had ample funds at practically no cost, incredibly low interest rates on their debts, and very little accountability to their shareholders. Over the past 10 years our Japanese partner has had far lower results and much lower growth than Lafarge Coppée.' Europeans demand higher profitability and a higher quality of life.

Jean-Louis Beffa of Saint-Gobain believes Europe will do best if it adapts the German approach to the industry/finance interface. 'What the Germans have understood for a long time is that the best way for the banks to be strong is to base themselves on strong industry. So the banks have to be smart enough to back industry first and help it become strong enough to live on.'

BALANCING SOCIAL RESPONSIBILITY WITH COMPETITIVENESS

Europe's social market economy is also taken as a 'given', especially when considered alongside the American and Japanese extremes. But to enable European business to compete and come out ahead, the directors believe that both the extent and the degree of social legislation need to be examined carefully in light of the lack of regulatory constraints in the United States and Japan.

'Looking down the road,' said Brian Goldthorp of Trafalgar House, 'the one thing whch may distinguish a successful from an unsuccessful corporation is the ability to gather together human resources and develop them in particular ways to create and use the strategic opportunities that the company sees: products, services, markets, etc. We have to protect the individual worker's rights, but I fear that Europe is becoming regimented and legalized, with too many "pigeonholes" that restrict managers and individuals from releasing their imagination and drive and responding to economic imperatives.'

He pointed to the Japanese use of autonomous working groups. 'Faced with a problem, they are allowed to configure themselves in any way they want in order to solve it. So there is no question of "we can't work more than 48 hours this week", or "we must have a meal break at noon", etc. They are given a very large degree of freedom to meet the needs and pressures of the situation.'

'One of the biggest risks we face in Europe is that the Community will overregulate, making the same mistake as at national levels in the past,' said Ernest Van Mourik Broekman of Shell. 'We must find a way to achieve a high level of differentiation within an open market in order to preserve flexibility — because flexibility will need to be one of our greatest competitive strengths.'

But even in business circles there is a great difference of opinion over the relative benefits of retaining flexibility versus achieving homogeneity of social benefits and regulations at a realistic and acceptable level. 'Once it becomes possible to create the legal entity of a European Company, authorized to open offices and factories everywhere it wants in Europe,' said Walter Schusser of Siemens, 'harmonization of social relations will inevitably have to follow.'

Many economic and social compromises will be required as European companies adjust to using the whole of the Single Market as their domestic base. Theoretically, companies will be able to reduce the number of production units used to supply Europe.

As Roland Berra of Hoffmann-La Roche pointed out, multinationals will no longer need to be in each country. 'But that can't be purely an economic decision: it must be a compromise which takes in both the social and economic consequences. All the social partners must face the fact that political stability has its cost. Rationalization at any cost might in the long-term be counterproductive if it is followed by a massive increase in unemployment, taxes, and instability.'

MAKING THE MOST OF THE SINGLE MARKET

Most companies who have wanted to sell across Europe in the past have managed to do so by surmounting the artificial trade barriers that were placed in their way. 'People used their sense of pragmatism to get over the obstacles,' said Viscount Etienne Davignon. 'Now that almost all of these barriers are down, companies have to be careful not to turn their former successful solutions into new obstacles. It is a paradox.

'Managers have become so used to dealing with the obstacles that they may not realize they need to stand back and look at the Single Market and the European Economic Area in a totally new manner, as if they were seeing it for the first time. By doing that, they will be able to discover the best and freshest approaches to take to meet their needs and reach their aims.

'Companies have the opportunities now to organize, produce, and operate in totally new ways that will fit the situation far better. Competitors from other parts of the globe realize this and are approaching European markets in this manner. If European companies do not, they will find that outsiders will beat them to their own market.'

BUILDING IN FLEXIBILITY

To meet and beat the competition, European companies are going to have to organize themselves in a way that enables them to change continuously and more rapidly. In order to achieve that, their employees will have to understand and be committed to the need to be flexible. People find it easier to be flexible if they can count on support, which is why it is now considered essential to teach individualistic European employees about teamwork and networking.

'Unilever has had more changes in the last six to eight years than in the entire 50 years before that,' remarked Floris Maljers. 'We've survived that because our people increasingly understand the need to be flexible in their organizational behaviour. We are now going in two new directions: project teams and an extended head office.

'With project teams we choose a group of people of all disciplines and departments who may have never worked together and say to them, for example: find (a) a new toothpaste which is (b) good for health and (c) can be launched all over Europe as soon as possible. The team members speak to people all over the company and work together under a project director to solve the problem. We call these "project teams" because we use people who are not normally doing that type of work and release the creativity of the new combinations of people, problems and ideas.

'The extended head office, I think, is another important organizational direction for European companies. We use this system to involve people in the operating units in headquarters decision making. For example, our central organization for detergents is located in Brussels, and consists of three full-time staff members there plus five part-time members who are based in the various countries and come to Brussels once a month for the decision-making process.'

These and other organizational designs will be used increasingly by European companies to enable them to take a 'glocal' approach to the Single Market: a central product line and basic marketing strategy informed by and tailored to local needs.

QUALITY IN PEOPLE AS WELL AS PRODUCTS AND PROCESSES

In responding to the challenges posed by the Japanese, many European companies have tried to raise the quality standards of their products and services. To make fuller use of the opportunities which the Single Market can provide, companies should also encourage their employees to engage in continuous personal development.

Managers will have to submit themselves to processes of Europeanization and internationalization. 'In the not too distant future,' said Paul Roettig of Austrian Industries, 'a Euromanager will be spending a week in Frankfurt, the next week in Paris, the next week in Brussels, and the week after that in Krakow. They will be opening themselves to all these cultures, and the best will be able to drink it all in and grow with it.'

Beyond that, because of the way knowledge and the complexity of life is increasing, the ERT directors believe that lifelong learning will become essential for everyone who wants to remain in the workforce. So people will have to learn how to learn, and build learning into their adult lives. They will not only have to be ready to learn new tasks, new fields, new specializations to enable themselves to keep up with the changes their companies will be instituting. They will also have to be prepared to open themselves to new levels of knowledge in the basic subject areas, like the sciences and mathematics.

CUSTOMER SERVICE AT EVERY LEVEL

As companies organize themselves for a total European approach to the Single Market, they will be able to discover new combinations and permutations of customer service. The most competitive will use them as a way to gain on the lead US and Japanese companies generally have in this area.

Hewlett-Packard is taking a totally European approach in terms of strategy, pricing and delivery, and almost moving away from a geographical viewpoint to an industry focus, said André Breukels. 'We ask ourselves, "How can we serve the European chemicals market, telecommunications market, the automobile market", etc. We are consolidating our "back-office" functions and using our national organizations for our direct customer interface.' Companies which have adopted this approach have seen strong benefits from it, he said.

It is an organizational system which is very similar to that used in the United States, Breukels explained. There Hewlett-Packard has one national organization with all the transaction centres that serve the entire country, and regional offices to serve the customers. As the European Community moves closer to a federal structure, he believes companies will be able to design a total European approach based on the US system.

In the opinion of Roland Berra of Hoffmann-La Roche, customer satisfaction will increasingly be linked to employee motivation. 'Often it is not the lack of training or knowledge that prevails,' he said, 'but the reluctance to please the customer. If the employees feel that the company — or the institution — does not treat them well, then they do not see why they should bother about the customer.'

EASTERN EUROPE

When we speak of the Single Market today we think in terms of the 18 countries within the European Economic Area: the 12 European Union member states plus six members of the European Free Trade Association. But to be geared for the 21st century, Euromanagers must expand their mental maps of their 'home base' to stretch from Lisbon to Vladivostock.

Moving into eastern Europe to invest, open subsidiaries, form joint ventures and sell products will require all the talent for diversity and tolerance that the western Europeans possess. There will be no magic wands to wave away the effects of 45 to 70 years of communist rule.

Many people think the best way to re-integrate the eastern Europeans is to teach them western practices as quickly as possible. Few expect the westerners to learn in return. But Paul Roettig of Austrian Industries, who works extensively with eastern Europe, disagrees. 'It would be very wrong of us to suppose that these people have to change without us changing as well. These people want our management and business tools, just as they've been taken by all the other countries of the world. But they want to guard their own mentality. Just like I want to remain Austrian.

'What we all need to do is to think European. But we musn't expect ourselves to unify to the point of the United States and Japan. Nowadays most Americans are American Americans. A Japanese is always a Japanese Japanese. But we will be Austrian Europeans, French Europeans, Czech Europeans and so on. And that will be the source of our true wealth.'

Justus Mische, who as Head of Human Resources of Hoechst has been heavily involved in questions of east-west integration, agrees that change must take place on both sides, but he believes there will be far more convergence from the east. 'This Marxist socialist dream still exists in the minds of intellectuals, but not in the hearts of those who had to live through it. I cannot believe that after their suffering they are going to reject our market-driven social system and seek a third road forward. Rather I see them trying to apply in a pragmatic fashion what they see practised in the west, realizing that what the west has is not perfect, but it works.'

There is a parallel between what is happening in the countries of eastern Europe today and the transitions undergone in those of Southeast Asia, according to Roland Berra of Hoffmann-La Roche. 'They all undergo a period of flux, where everything is chaotic while they change from the old system to the new. People are lost. But once the start is made, the evolution is phenomenal.

'Within a period of 15 years I saw Indonesia pass from practically the Middle Ages to a modernism equal to Europe today. And it was all done by the market economy. That's why I think the great task of European governments and business today is not to create schools in which to teach the easterners, but to help them create companies, either through investments or by buying their products.

'It is only after they have tasted the fruits of the market that they will be hungry to learn what we can teach them through courses. And then they will learn very quickly. I saw it happen all over Asia. Schools began sprouting like mushrooms in every field — accounting, marketing, languages — and everyone began taking courses at night. And after several years, the managers were as well trained as many in western Europe. And I expect the same thing to happen in eastern Europe, because the people there have a good educational base and deep inside they know how to work if they have an opportunity and are motivated to do so.'

When the eastern Europeans are ready to learn about managing companies in a market economy, will they be taught the American, the Japanese, or the European management model?

12
Euromanagement skills

There are some key principles which European managers can learn which will enable them to make their companies more competitive as they cope with the enormous changes European business is living through. These are:

- the capacity to change;
- an open mindset;
- the ability to learn from others, adapting their ways to your own situation;
- an entrepreneurial spirit;
- communication skills, including other languages.

They are all basic attitudes which have to become part of the way managers look at the world before they can be put to use. The formal precepts can be taught through books and courses, but even knowledge of a foreign language remains superficial if you dont *use* it to deal with life. To own these attitudes and make them part of their core personality, managers have to turn an internal key deep inside them to the 'open' position.

This is a much harder task than learning how to use the latest management systems. But it is well within the range of the possible for any European manager who chooses to do it. Look at the list again: the key characteristics required today are the same ones that flourished in Renaissance times. If Europeans could do it 500 years ago as they crawled out of the Middle Ages without the aid of 20th century knowledge and technology, surely European managers can do it now.

THE CAPACITY TO CHANGE

To cope successfully with business life in Europe today, it is essential for managers to develop the capacity to change. As we said in Chapter 1, change has become a way of life in business all over the modern world. For companies who intend to survive, competition and technological progress leave no alternative. But business in Europe is facing far more stress, for major change is occurring on all its fronts at once: economic, political and social.

'We have to learn to live in ambiguity, in uncertainty, even in the sciences,' advised Roland Berra of Hoffmann-La Roche. 'We have passed that period of euphoria where we believed that thanks to science we could solve all the problems. Realizing it is not so is painful.'

'All the parameters are changing very quickly, and we must adapt to that,' said Didier Pineau-Valencienne, CEO of Groupe Schneider. 'Until recently we have been in a very long period of growth. Now we must prepare ourselves and our executives to manage periods of strong decline as well as growth. We must build companies that can ride the waves. To do that many companies must also develop a long-term technological strategy. That means directors will have to be capable of taking options in areas they do not know well, committing huge amounts of money to develop technologies that will come onto the market in 10 years' time.'

According to José-Alberto Blanco Losada of Telefónica, 'the secret does not lie in the mastery and application of techniques or theories alone. They have to be combined with the humanities and channelled through the humanism which is at the base of European culture. You have to remember to keep people at the centre of your thinking. That is how you learn to accept change and adapt to it by changing with it.'

AN OPEN MINDSET

Managers can cope with change more easily if their minds are open: ready to drink in new or just different ideas and approaches. Europeans are predisposed to this through their exposure to diverse cultures, but the characteristic now has to be developed to make greater use of it. To compete successfully in the Single Market, managers will find they have to destroy the stereotypes, prejudices and boundaries in their minds and open the borders of their thinking.

'It will be important for managers to think European, because that will be their domestic market. They will have to have the capacity to adapt and synthesize the different systems they see and to make products that are valid for all of Europe — because that will prove to be 65 per cent of their market,' said André Leysen of Agfa-Gevaert.

'To manage properly in Europe today, I think a manager has to have been in a situation outside of his own environment for a long time or several times,' commented Wisse Dekker of Philips. 'I moved 14 times, which I don't advise everyone doing. But I do think you must know Europe and you must know about Japan and the United States. The international elements are very important for your development and training.'

Such experience gives a manager a tremendous advantage, noted Bertrand Collomb. 'It enables you to comprehend different cultures, and thus understand that although there may be techniques which are effectively universal, they cannot be applied simply — you must first understand the context of a situation. Many times you can tailor the techniques to the situation, but sometimes they are simply inapplicable.'

THE ABILITY TO LEARN FROM OTHERS

The Single Market will give managers tremendous opportunities to work with and compete against their fellow Europeans. While there are strong similarities in the way European managers behave in business, many interesting differences remain. The diversity will enable everyone to learn from the best practices in other countries.

Companies must also sift through business practices in the United States and Japan and absorb the best of what they see, said Brian Goldthorp of Trafalgar House. 'From American corporations I think we should learn their ability to look globally and their entrepreneurial flair. From Japanese corporations I think the most important thing to learn is their willingness and ability to look at themselves and at their markets and ask the question "What is it that the market is going to require in 10 and 20 years' time, and what do we need to do about ourselves, our products and our services to meet that?" Then in a very dispassionate, wide-ranging, ruthless way they change, abandon and create products and services and configure themselves in the way that is needed. I think there are very few European companies who are able and willing to do that. But we shall have to learn how.'

'A global strategy doesn't necessarily mean you understand more,' remarked Pehr Gyllenhammar of Volvo. 'You could have the ambition to be everywhere without understanding very much of what is going on. To understand you have to respect and you have to study.

'What the Japanese have done is studied us and studied the Americans. And you can see the results. We have not studied the Japanese, not carefully. But they are very successful, so we should study them and try to understand why. "Japan bashing" — claiming they succeed because they are unfair — is dangerous and wrong. In trade negotiations you have to be tough, but when it comes to developing your business, it is much more important to open your eyes and ears and try to learn.'

'The more you operate in an international manner, the more open you become and the more you adapt yourself, but there will always be cultural barriers and frontiers that must be taken into account', said Walter Schusser of Siemens. 'Take the theme of quality circles, for example. It is a very good idea to unleash people's initiative, creativity and potential. But it cannot work here in the same form in which it works in Japan. We have to develop our own forms, based far more on the individual.'

AN ENTREPRENEURIAL SPIRIT

Entrepreneurial flair is something you are born with; it cannot come from books, according to most entrepreneurs. But if the spark of the spirit exists within someone, it can certainly be expanded and developed.

'Americans enjoy doing business,' said Brian Goldthorp. 'They like putting together deals. They are quick, imaginative, use lateral thinking. We are very cumbersome and ponderous by comparison.'

But the Japanese are also slower than the Americans, remarked Jean-Louis Beffa of Saint-Gobain. He thinks the explanation is to be found in the fear of failure. Beffa believes the way to create a more entrepreneurial spirit within European companies is to change the environment that surrounds risk taking. 'In European companies, taking risks means facing the possibility of failure, and failure is not easily accepted. In Japan, a manager who does *not* take a development risk is viewed very badly; people accept far more easily those who have taken a risk but had a bad result.' In the United States, too, failed risks are a normal part of life. One simply starts again.

Good marketing and customer service develop naturally from a trading and entrepreneurial spirit. Once again, techniques are not sufficient. They have to be applied by managers who keep people at the centre of their thinking.

COMMUNICATION SKILLS

'Euromanagers of today and tomorrow have to understand that they will spend much more of their time communicating than their predecessors', said Bertrand Collomb of Lafarge Coppée. 'In order to lead well, they have to be able to communicate well, whatever their position.'

Better communication skills have been on company shopping lists for the past decade. For the top-down/bottom-up information flow to work, managers must know how to communicate verbally and in writing with people inside their company, as well as clients and the general public.

Good communication skills are also a necessary ingredient of teamwork. As the business climate becomes increasingly complex, companies will increasingly depend on teams for problem solving. 'It is not very difficult to create a team of engineers or a team of accountants, or even lawyers,' said Theodore Papalexopoulos of Titan Cement. 'But it is terribly difficult to create a team that works well with one lawyer, one engineer, one chemist and one accountant. It seems to me that young managers do not know how to communicate sufficiently with people outside their own special field. It's as if one were speaking Chinese and the other French. Often I find the solution is to inject into the team someone who is professionally bilingual — for example an engineer with an MBA. I think the problem stems from excessive specialization at too early an age. I find more and more that the keystones to my solutions are the people who can form bridges between the professionals and enable the group to communicate.'

The Single Market adds multiple dimensions to the communication matrix, for now managers need to learn to communicate in several languages. As André Leysen commented, 'It's those who speak the languages who dominate Europe.'

When a Dane and a Greek and a Czech meet, they may have to speak in French or German or English — or mixtures of all three — to communicate. And they do. This is part of what Europe is all about. It is interesting to recall that for the interviews quoted in this book, many of the CEOs and directors spoke continuously for more than an hour in their second or third language. It is doubtful whether the directors of the top companies in the United States or Japan would be able to do that — because they do not need to.

'I think it is indispensable for European managers to recognize that we are European — not Japanese and not American,' said Roland Berra of Hoffmann-La Roche. 'It is time for us all to think deeply about our qualities and strengths, how to mobilize people through them. And we have to discover that ourselves.

'We must continue to learn the best practices of the Americans and the Japanese, but it is time for European managers to stop copying from them blindly because their way of thinking doesn't necessarily apply to our situation. Above all, we must shed this almost inferiority complex about ourselves compared to the Japanese and Americans.'

This is only one of the reasons why the directors would like to see European managers being trained more in business schools that consider Europe as the domestic market.

BUSINESS SCHOOLS FOR THE SINGLE MARKET

There was remarkable agreement among the ERT directors on what and how they would like business schools in Europe to be teaching. The first thing they want is European-based management training. That means a European curriculum taught by a European faculty. To that curriculum the directors want to see added the best approaches and methods used by US and Japanese companies, and ways to integrate those into European business practices.

'Those who teach should be more international in their contacts, in their training, in their experience, and they should be able to base their teaching on real experience, real facts,' commented Jean-Louis Beffa of Saint-Gobain. 'For example, I would like to see teachers who have spent time in Japan as well as America, integrating what they have learned and experienced there into material drawn from Europe.'

'At the moment,' said Brian Goldthorp, 'I see an awful lot of narrow focus and nationalism in the teaching of business schools. In the future, I would not send any rising development executive to any institution that could not demonstrate to me that it had, first of all, a European focus, a European strategy and a European faculty. Beyond that, I want a world focus as well.'

To help create a truly European approach, the directors would like to see the students at business schools drawn from all the countries and mixed together. This would help the schools to teach and talk about the European population, instead of just one nationality. Strong links with universities and business schools in other countries are also being encouraged. Because every director interviewed believes young rising executives in Europe must have experience in countries outside their national environment, they would like to see this as a built-in feature of more courses. This includes Japan and the United States as well as other European countries.

Personal skills

Another strong plea from the directors is for business schools to put more emphasis on the 'human elements': the behavioural sciences, sociology, psychology and personal development. 'Teaching is turned far too strongly in a technical sense. It cannot continue like that. It must include more of the social aspects of business and of life,' said Justus Mische of Hoechst. 'We are getting very intelligent young people from the universities, but they don't know how to work in a team. And no wonder. They pass their whole life in university in a very individualistic fashion, and come to us trained to work in an important sector of research, which is incredibly complicated and specialized. But they have difficulties in communicating inside the firm on an everyday basis. They were not trained in social techniques, in how to solve a problem with people who have a different point of view. If the universities and business schools do not develop this, then the companies have to. It is one of our most important training efforts at Hoechst.'

'Hoffmann-La Roche has been doing just that for some years,' said Roland Berra. 'We now attach a great deal of importance to subjects which were not a priority in the past, especially for professionals. All of our managers — irrespective of the area in which they work — are expected to develop very good skills in managing people. They learn to ask themselves how people function, what motivates them, how they learn, what makes them come up with new ideas, take risks, etc. They are also being trained in marketing — to get a feel for customers' needs, and in finance to develop business sense.

'The demands on specialists — particularly on researchers — have also changed. Increasingly they have to work in teams, to communicate, to anticipate the long-term impact and value of their discoveries. Being specialized in and of itself is no longer enough today.'

To make it obvious that personal skills are vitally important in business today, Jean-Louis Beffa of Saint-Gobain suggests that students are evaluated on them as well as on their intellectual performance. 'I think teachers should not hesitate to talk to their students about their personalities and social skills, their personal development, and to help them assess these areas honestly.'

'The Anglo-Saxon school systems are far better at this than continental ones,' said Theodore Papalexopoulos of Titan Cement, 'because of the way students are valued and the freedom of expression they are allowed in the classroom. A student in an Anglo-Saxon university feels nearly the equal of the professor. But a student on the continent tends to be treated like a pawn. And like pawns, they are expected to sit there, listen and take notes — not speak. But from a young age in Anglo-Saxon schools children are encouraged to speak, taught to debate, obliged to argue and discuss from different points of view.

'This has a remarkable effect. By the time they achieve their diplomas, the good Anglo-Saxon students are ready and interested to participate. By comparison, students from many Continental schools are "flat" from the point of view of internal dynamism. It has been ironed out of them.'

Lifelong learning

Because the ERT directors are committed to the concept of lifelong learning, they would like to see business schools and universities design courses for managers of all ages. For them, MBAs taken at age 30 can be even more valuable than those earned at age 24. By 30 years of age the young managers have practical experience in their first degree subject and have lived in the realistic daily world of business. The breadth and depth of knowledge that they bring to the courses enable them to derive far greater value from what they are being taught.

The directors realize that for managers to meet the demands that the changing scene in Europe will make on them, more time and money will have to be spent on their education and training. They believe business schools and universities in Europe can satisfy those needs only if they provide the European and international focus to match the reality European managers will be seeing from their desks.

13
Reconciling forces

Europe is described in many ways. When most people consider it they remark on its diversity. What we have shown you in this book are the underlying and emerging similarities.

European managers are more similar than you might expect, but also just as diverse as you suspect. This cultural diversity is Europe's unique wealth. Learning to integrate the diversity by combining the best practices of each nation will be Europe's strategic strength.

For commercial purposes, the domestic market of European companies now extends across the 18 countries of the European Economic Area. Political and economic forces are already working to turn central and eastern Europe into the neighbouring free trade area.

Most companies will not be able to stay snug and comfortable in their own local or national markets. Competition will come pouring in from outside. So managers will have to take their companies onto the European level. Many will then use the Single Market as a springboard onto world markets.

A EUROPEAN MANAGEMENT MODEL

What are the traits European managers will need to face these challenges successfully? The interviews with directors on which this book is based revealed a profile of characteristics which we have called an evolving European management model. It captures the 'best practices' shared by top directors of many of Europe's biggest companies:

❏ **Manage international diversity**: respect and appreciate it, learn from it, milk it, and integrate it to the extent needed to achieve

flexibility and enhance your company's ability to ride the waves of change.
- **Lead as well as manage**: work with the company's employees as colleagues and partners, not as 'them' to your managerial 'us'.
- **Play your social role**: recognize that European companies have a social role to play as well as an economic one, but do not allow it to endanger the life of the company, for that would be against the interests of all its stakeholders: the workforce, the managers, the shareholders, the creditors, the suppliers, the customers, and the wider community which it serves.
- **Continue to think long-term**: but learn to pair long-term planning with short-term flexibility.
- **Recognize and use the benefits of Europeans' inherent individuality**: understand that young people today seek involvement in their work, commitment to their companies and fuller development of their abilities, but that they also seek balanced lives and will not be 'owned' by their jobs. Profit from the male/female approach: make the most of the women in the human resource pool, and teach the men how to develop the 'senses' sides of their characters which are needed for the new team style of business organization.
- **Combine a world outlook with global strategies**: learn to distinguish between situations that require differentiation and those which are best suited to a more uniform approach.

Business in Europe today is facing formidable change and challenges. But it has the chance and the ability to ride the waves of change into a new era. As it does, the European management model described in this book will continue to evolve.

Watching the currents of the present economic recession, we suspect that the European social system will also undergo change and evolve. An important question is whether it will still be moulded by the basic European values.

RECONCILING CONTRADICTORY FORCES

When we discussed the 'American dream', 'Japan, Inc.', and the 'European view of the world', we spoke of the contradictions within the European view and how the current economic recession is putting some of them into conflict. Perhaps some solutions can be found, as in Renaissance times, by revisiting the wisdom of the cradle of European civilization.

The ancient Greeks had a tradition of reconciling apparently opposite forces. So it is possible to have:

- European *and* British, French, German . . . ;
- social responsibility *and* profits;
- long-term planning *and* short-term flexibility;
- diversity *and* integration;
- world outlook *and* global strategies;
- leadership *and* management;
- individuality *and* teamwork;
- a balanced life *and* commitment to the company.

As the Greeks learned, reconciled forces are far stronger. If managers choose to make the effort to harness the positive forces in Europe today and forge them into a new integrated power, we shall indeed find we are living in a Renaissance of European management.

Appendix:
The Participants in the Study*

Agfa-Gevaert NV — André Leysen
Agfa-Gevaert specializes in chemical and electronic imaging systems. With headquarters in Mortsel, Belgium, the company has 26,000 employees worldwide and in 1992 had an annual turnover of BF140 billion.

André Leysen is Chairman of the company's Supervisory Board. He began his career at the age of 25 in his own private shipping company, and joined Agfa-Gevaert in 1978. The following year he became its CEO.

In addition to sitting on the boards and advisory committees of nine other major companies and international organizations, André Leysen writes socio-economic and political essays, is a Member and Past Chairman of Board of the Royal Belgian Opera House, and is present Chairman of the Rubens house in Antwerp, the city where he was born.

---

* Directors and managers from other companies also participated in the study, but asked not to be quoted and not to have their names included in this list.

Amorim Group — Américo Amorim
The Amorim Group is a Portugal-based holding company whose operations are divided into five main groups: natural resources, general manufacturing activities, financial services, real estate and tourism, and information systems.

Américo Ferreira de Amorim is President of the Group. Active in a wide range of industrial and trade organizations as well as being Chairman of the Board of the Circulo de Cultura Musical, he has received many honours, including being named 'best Portuguese entrepreneur of the year'.

Austrian Industries AG — Paul F Roettig
Austrian Industries was the biggest company in Austria, being a conglomerate of 700 subsidiaries with a total workforce of 86,000. The Group is divided into four sectors: oils and chemicals, steel, aluminium, and technologies. Totally state owned, the Group is now in the process of being restructured and privatized.

Paul F Roettig was the Senior Vice President of Human Resources of Austrian Industries from 1987 to 1992. Before that he worked for 17 years with Exxon in human resources, marketing and corporate planning, with posts in Europe, Africa and the US. He now chairs the Salzburg Management Institute and lectures at American and Austrian universities.

He and his wife have two adopted daughters, born in Bangladesh, and the family's weekend hobby is an old farmhouse, where they produce their own cider and keep bees. Mr Roettig has published two books and numerous articles.

Robert Bosch GmbH — Hans L Merkle
Robert Bosch manufactures automotive equipment, communications technology, capital goods and consumer goods. The company has 160,000 employees worldwide and in 1992 had a turnover of DM34 billion.

Hans L Merkle joined the Bosch Group in 1958, and later became Chairman of the Supervisory and Management Boards of Robert Bosch GmbH (Germany). He is now a Managing Partner of the governing body of the entire Bosch Group.

British Petroleum — Robert Horton
British Petroleum operates in 70 countries with 95,000 employees. The company has three main sectors of activity: exploration and production of oil and gas; trading, shipping, refining, distribution and marketing of crude oil and petroleum products; and manufacture of a range of petrochemicals and intermediate products. In 1992 British Petroleum's annual turnover was £33 billion.

Robert Horton is the former Chairman and CEO of British Petroleum, a position he took after having spent most of his career in the oil industry. He is now Executive Chairman of Railtrack, a government-owned company which is charged with owning and operating the railway infrastructure in the United Kingdom.

Education is one of Robert Horton's special interests, and he is Chancellor of the University of Kent, having been educated at St Andrew's University in Scotland and at the Massachusetts Institute of Technology in the US. His other interests include opera and collecting art and antiquarian books.

BSN Group — Antoine Riboud, Daniel Lefort

Manufacturers of foodstuffs and food packaging, the BSN Group has 60,000 employees worldwide and in 1992 had an annual turnover of FF70.8 billion.

Antoine Riboud is Chairman and Chief Executive Officer of the BSN Group, and is also President of Mechaniver and Gervais Danone. Born in 1918 in Lyon, Antoine Riboud received a diploma from the Ecole Supérieure de Commerce in Paris and began his career in the glass industry at the age of 23. In 1943 he joined one of the three firms from which BSN was formed, and remained within the group. He was named Président-Directeur-Général of BSN-Gervais Danone in 1973 and since then has continued to head the entire BSN group as it grew.

Antoine Riboud has been a member of the ERT since 1988 and is also a Member of the Board of l'Association Progrès et Environnement.

Daniel Lefort is the BSN Group Directeur-Général of Human Resources.

The Coca-Cola Company — Ralph H Cooper

The Coca-Cola Company is the world's leading soft drink company, serving 685 million drinks per day in more than 195 countries. The company has about 32,000 employees worldwide and in 1992 had an annual turnover of $13.73 billion.

Ralph H Cooper is Senior Vice-President of The Coca-Cola Company and President of its European Community Group, with operating responsibility for all the EC countries. He joined the company in 1965 at its Atlanta, Georgia, headquarters, after receiving his BS degree in chemical engineering and an MBA. In Atlanta, he progressed through a series of positions which included market planning, and in 1971 transferred to the company's Foods Division. He moved to London in 1979 as Division Marketing Director of the Northern European Division of the Coca-Cola Export Corporation, and in 1988 was appointed President of Coca-Cola Northern Europe.

Appointed to his current position in 1990, Ralph Cooper is based again in Atlanta. He is married with two daughters, and enjoys flyfishing as his hobby.

Daimler-Benz — Claudia Schlossberger

The Daimler-Benz Group is composed of four divisions with activities in motor vehicles, electrotechnical and rail systems, microelectronics, aircraft, space and defence systems, and software. It has more than 375,000 employees worldwide, and in 1992 had an annual turnover of DM98 million.

Claudia Schlossberger is a Senior Manager in Corporate Executive Development. Educated in Munich, Moscow and Montpelier in Slavonic linguistics and Economics, she joined Daimler-Benz in 1982 and was appointed to her current position ten years later. Dr Schlossberger is married and has two children. Her favourite leisure pursuits are literature, swimming and being with her family.

Fiat SpA — Umberto Agnelli, John Kirschen, Vittorio Tesio, Laura Bonisconti

The Fiat Group was founded in Turin in northern Italy in July 1899. Within four years the company was exporting passenger cars to the United States. By 1905 Fiat had opened dealerships in Australia, and by 1907 Fiat cars were being manufactured under licence in Austria.

Today the Fiat Group operates in 63 countries, with 285,000 employees working in some 1100 companies. They are grouped into 16 operating sectors, including automobiles, commercial vehicles, vehicle components, tractors, earth-moving machines, civil engineering, railcars and rolling stock, aviation components, and financial services. In 1992 the Fiat Group's annual turnover was L59 billion.

Umberto Agnelli is the former Vice Chairman of Fiat. Before taking on his responsibilities with the company, he acquired experience with other companies in the Fiat Group. He returned to Turin in 1968, when he assumed charge of Fiat's International Operations. From 1970 to 1980 he was Managing Director of Fiat.

Umberto Agnelli is also Chairman or a Member of the Board of a large number of other Italian and international companies, industry associations and trade organizations, and chairs the ERT Working group on Infrastructure.

John Kirschen is Vice President of Fiat Europe.

Vittorio Tesio is in charge of Personnel Planning and Management Development for the Fiat Group.

Laura Bonisconti, an economist who specialized in the labour market and socio-economic planning, joined Fiat in 1977. She was appointed Head of the Group's Industrial Relations Research Office in 1988, and in 1993 became responsible also for Internal Communications.

Hewlett-Packard SA — André Breukels
Hewlett-Packard's main sectors of activity are computer and equipment systems, test and measurement equipment, medical and analytical products, and electronic components.

André Breukels was born in the Netherlands and joined Hewlett-Packard in 1961, at the age of 23. After a series of posts in Europe as Sales Manager, Benelux Area Manager and Country General Manager in Denmark, he was appointed General Manager for the Northern European Region and then Personnel Director for Europe. André Breukels is now Personnel Director for Hewlett-Packard's American Division.

Hoechst AG — Justus Mische, Monika Düssel
Hoechst AG is a Germany-based company with fully integrated production, sales, and research facilities in more than ten other countries, bringing its worldwide workforce to nearly 178,000. The Group manufactures chemicals, dyes, fibres, polymers, and pharmaceutical products, and in 1992 had an annual turnover of nearly DM46 billion.

Justus Mische is a Member of the Board in charge of Personnel. Born in 1938, he has been with Hoechst AG since 1958, when he entered its vocational commercial training programme. He then studied Business Management at the University of Berlin and returned to Hoechst's Fibre Sales department. In 1988 he transferred to Personnel and Staff Welfare, and in 1990 was appointed to his current position. Justus Mische is married with three children.

Monika Düssel joined Hoechst AG in 1988 as Manager of International Affairs for the Central Office of the Board of Management.

Hoffmann-La Roche AG — Roland Berra
F Hoffmann-La Roche Ltd produces pharmaceuticals, vitamins and fine chemicals, diagnostics, fragrances and flavours. It has an annual turnover of SF14.5 million and more than 56,300 employees worldwide, with headquarters in Basle.

Roland Berra, Head of Corporate Executive Resources, has had more than 30 years' experience working with European and American corporations, half of which has been spent in Asia. His main career has been in marketing and general management. He moved to his current post in 1986, where he is responsible for ensuring the development of a powerful pool of talent within the entire Hoffman-La Roche corporation.

Itochu Europe plc — Hiroshi Wakabayashi

Itochu Europe Plc is a general trading company. It has 470 employees, 127 of whom are based in the United Kingdom. It is part of the Itochu Group, which has 10,000 employees worldwide and in 1992 had an annual turnover of $8 billion.

Hiroshi Wakabayashi is Group Chief Executive of the Development and Investment Management Group of Itochu Europe. He first joined Itochu in Japan in 1964, and was its representative in Vienna from 1971–74. He returned to Japan for the next ten years and then became General Manager of the Office for Project Information and Co-ordination of Itochu Europe. From 1989–92 he was Assistant to the President of the company, and in 1993 was appointed to his current post, which is situated in London.

Hiroshi Wakabayashi is married, has two daughters and enjoys classical music and golf as his leisure pursuits.

Lafarge Coppée — Bertrand Collomb
Lafarge Coppée is one of the world's foremost producers of construction materials — cement, plasterboard, concrete and aggregates, paints and coatings — and is also active in biotechnology, specializing in food additives and seeds. The Group was founded more than 100 years ago, and today has more than 500 affiliates in 35 countries. Worldwide, Lafarge Coppée has 30,000 employees and in 1992 it had an annual turnover of FF30 billion.

Bertrand Collomb is Chairman and CEO of Lafarge Coppée. Born in Lyon in 1942, he was educated at Ecole Polytechnique and Ecole des Mines in Paris, and earned a law degree in France as well as a Doctorate in Management from the University of Texas. After his studies he worked with the French government in various posts, and founded and managed the Centre for Management Research at the Ecole Polytechnique.

He joined Lafarge Coppée in 1975 in France, as regional manager of cement operations, and soon became President and CEO of Ciments Lafarge France. In 1983 he was appointed CEO of Orsan, the group's biotechnology company, and in 1987 was appointed CEO of the Group's North American arm as well as a Group Director. He became Vice-Chairman and CEO of the Lafarge Coppée Group in January 1989, and was appointed its Chairman eight months later.

Bertrand Collomb is a member of the European Round Table, a former Chairman of the ERT Working Group on Education and Vice-Chairman of the World Industry Council for the Environment. He is married with three children and in his leisure time enjoys horse riding, tennis and hunting.

Lyonnaise des Eaux-Dumez — Jérôme Monod, Marc Fornacciari
Lyonnaise des Eaux-Dumez is a worldwide group of 720 companies which has its main activities in water and waste management and treatment, energy and heating equipment, construction of buildings and public works, and the management of public services. The Group was formed in 1990 by a merger of two companies, each of which was more than 100 years old. Lyonnaise des Eaux-Dumez today has 130,000 employees worldwide and in 1992 had a turnover of FF90 billion.

Jérôme Monod has been Chairman and Président Directeur-Général of Lyonnaise des Eaux-Dumez since 1990. He also sits on the Boards of eleven other companies, is a member of the Consultative Council of the Banque de France, and is Chairman of the European Round Table.

Born in Paris, he earned a liberal arts degree from Wesleyan University in the US, graduate degrees in law and in literature in France, was graduated from the Institute d'Etudes Politiques in Paris, and trained as a senior public servant at the Ecole Nationale d'Administration. Jérôme Monod began his career as a senior staff member in a cabinet office and in 1975–76 was Chief of Staff to Prime Minister Jacques Chirac. He then held posts in politics, academia and business before joining Lyonnaise des Eaux as its Vice-Chairman in 1979. The following year he was named Chairman and CEO of the company. When it merged with Dumez in September 1990, he was named Chairman of the Group.

Jérôme Monod is married to a lawyer, and they have three children.

Marc Fornacciari is Director of Planning for Lyonnaise des Eaux-Dumez.

Nestlé Ltd — Helmut O Maucher

Nestlé is one of the biggest producers of food products in the world, and also has interests in cosmetics, pharmaceuticals and petfoods. The company traces its origins back to 1866, with the opening of Europe's first condensed milk factory in Cham, Switzerland. Now based in Vevey, the Nestlé Group has 438 factories and 218,000 employees worldwide. In 1992 the Group's annual turnover was SF54.5 million.

Helmut O Maucher is Chairman of the Board and CEO of the Nestlé Group, the company with which he has spent his entire career. Born in Eisenharz, Germany, he entered commercial apprenticeship at the Nestlé factory there after completing secondary school. He then transferred to the company's offices in Frankfurt and while holding various positions, studied for a BA in Business Administration and Economics at Frankfurt University.

From 1964 Helmut Maucher held a number of management positions with Nestlé Gruppe Deutschland, and in 1975 was appointed its President and CEO. In October 1980 he transferred to Nestlé in Vevey, as Executive Vice President of the Group. The following year he became CEO of the Group, and in June 1990 was also named Chairman of the Board. Helmut Maucher sits on the Boards and Councils of seven other companies.

The Nokia Group — Simo Vuorilehto, Kirsi-Marja Kuivalainen

The Nokia Group, based in Helsinki, comprises five business groups which specialize in consumer electronics, mobile phones, telecommunications, electrical cables and machinery, tyres and electrical power. The Group has operations in 36 countries, with 26,500 employees worldwide, and generates more than 70 per cent of its sales outside Finland. In 1992 the annual turnover of the Nokia group was Mk18 billion.

Simo Vuorilehto is the former CEO and Executive Board Chairman of the Nokia Group. Born in Finland in 1930, he earned his Master of Science degree from Helsinki University of Technology and spent nearly his entire career working on the production side of Finnish companies. In 1976 he became President of Nokia's Forest Industry Group and also Director of the Central Association of the Finnish Forestry Industry. Seven years later Simo Vuorilehto was appointed Executive Vice President of Operations of the Nokia Group, and in 1986 became its President and Chief Operating Officer. He was appointed CEO and Chairman of the Group Executive Board in 1988, and retired in May 1992.

While CEO of the Nokia Group, Simo Vuorilehto sat on the boards of more than 10 other companies. He is a member of more than 25 professional, cultural and community organizations, a Captain in Finland's military forces, and is a Knight first class of the Order of the Lion of Finland. He is married and has three children.

Kirsi-Marja Kuivalainen is Vice President of the Nokia Group, in charge of Human Resources. She earned her Master of Science degree in production economics in 1976 from Helsinki University of Technology, and from 1975 to 1988 worked for the Nestlé Corporation in human resources management, attaining the post of Corporate Assistant Vice President.

She then joined one of the Nokia Group companies as Vice President for Human Resources and within two years was appointed to her present position in the Group. Kirsi-Marja Kuivalainen is also a member of the Council for Higher Education in Finland and a Board Member of Employment Conditions Abroad. She is married to a research professor and they have two children.

NTT Europe Ltd. — Kageo Nakano
NTT Europe is the London-based operation of the Nippon Telephone and Telegraph Corporation. The telecommunications group has 242,300 employees worldwide and in 1992 had an annual turnover of Y6.5 billion. The European company concentrates on establishing relationships with carriers and Japanese users of global telecommunications networks, and investigating possible joint ventures.

Kageo Nakano is Managing Director of NTT Europe. Born in Tokyo, he graduated from Tokyo University's Faculty of Law in 1962, entered NTT the same year, and has spent his career mainly in commercial activities. He has a wife and two children. As leisure activities Kageo Nakano enjoys tennis and plays a Japanese musical instrument.

Petrofina SA — François Cornélis
Petrofina is engaged in all aspects of exploration and production of petroleum and petroleum products, operating in 14 countries, with exploration in 20 countries. Petrofina is also active in chemicals and paints. The company has its headquarters in Belgium and 15,500 employees worldwide. In 1992 it had a turnover of BF556 billion.

François Cornélis is CEO of Petrofina. Born in Brussels in 1949, he graduated from the University of Louvain as a mechanical engineer and entered Petrofina's data processing centre as a Systems Engineer two years later. He became manager of supply and shipping operations of Petrofina UK in London in 1979, became the Group Co-ordinator of refining and supply operations in Brussels in 1981, and in 1983 was appointed Vice President and Special Assistant to the President of American Petrofina in Dallas.

Two years later François Cornélis returned to Brussels as Assistant to the Chairman of the company. The following year he was named Executive Director, and in 1990 he was appointed Chief Executive Officer of Petrofina SA. He is the father of four children.

Philips — Wisse Dekker, Regina Matthijsen, Willem H J Guitink
Philips Electronics, which had a turnover of US$32.3 billion in 1992, began as a small light bulb factory founded by a young engineer in 1891 in the town of Eindhoven, in the Netherlands. Today the company's key activities are lighting, electronic components, consumer electronics, communications systems, industrial electronics, and medical systems. Still based in Eindhoven, Philips Electronics now has 275 factories in 43 countries, research laboratories in five countries, sales organizations in 60 countries, and marketing and service outlets in 150 countries — bringing its workforce to a total of 250,000 employees.

Wisse Dekker is Chairman of the Supervisory Board of Philips. He joined the company in 1948 at the age of 24, and was sent to Indonesia to work in various positions there for the next eight years. After returning to the Netherlands, he was appointed, in 1966, General Director of the Philips Organization in the Far East. Six years later he joined the management of Philips in the UK and soon became its Chairman. He was named President and Chairman of the Board of Management of the Philips Group in 1982 and became Chairman of the Supervisory Board in 1986.

In addition to being the joint founder and former Chairman of the European Round Table, for several years Wisse Dekker was Extraordinary Professor of International Business Management at Leiden University. He is married with two children and four grandchildren, and enjoys golfing and reading as his principal leisure pursuits.

Regina Matthijsen-Sebbel is Head of the International Industrial Relations Department of Philips. Born in Germany, she studied, taught and worked in England, France, Germany, Switzerland and the US before settling in the Netherlands. She holds degrees in languages and business administration from the universities of Geneva and Düsseldorf, and is the author of several publications in the fields of national and international labour relations. She joined Philips International in 1978 in the Personnel and Industrial Relations Department, and was appointed to her current post in 1987.

Regina Matthijsen-Sebbel is married, has two children, and enjoys skiing, music, and the theatre.

Willem H J Guitink is Corporate Director of Management Training and Education for Philips International. Having studied law in

Leiden and economics in London, he worked in Europe and the United States before joining Philips in 1964. Over the next 20 years he was appointed to a series of positions in marketing, product management, logistics, project management and plant management, with postings in 13 different countries. He became Corporate Human Resources Manager in 1984 and was appointed to his current position in 1989.

Willem Guitink is married with two children and has a wide variety of hobbies, including Olympic honours hockey, tennis, cricket, golf and gardening.

Pilkington — Sir Antony Pilkington
The Pilkington Group is one of the world's largest producers of flat and safety glass, and also has interests in ophthalmics, optronics and insulation. Founded as a small family business in 1826 in Lancashire, the Group now has some 90 operating subsidiaries in the United Kingdom and over 200 subsidiary and related companies operating in 30 other countries, bringing its number of employees worldwide to 37,000. In 1993 the turnover of the Pilkington Group was more than £2.5 billion.

Sir Antony Pilkington is the fifth generation of his family to run the company. He joined the company in 1959, and became its Chairman in 1980.

Pirelli SpA — Jacopo Vittorelli, Gavino Manca, Silvia Petocchi
Pirelli SpA is the most geographically diversified Italy-based multinational. Based in Milan with commercial operations and R&D centres on every continent, the Group has 65,000 employees and 144 factories which produce tyres, cables, motor vehicle and industrial components, and consumer products. In 1992 Pirelli had an annual turnover of L8.25 billion.

Jacopo Vittorelli is the former Deputy Chairman of the Pirelli Group. Born in Venice in 1923, he earned a degree in civil engineering from Bologna University and began his career with Pirelli immediately afterwards. He worked in the tyre sector in Italy, the United Kingdom, Spain and Greece, and in 1965 was appointed Managing Director of Pirelli's subsidiary in Brazil. In 1971 Jacopo Vittorelli became General Manager of Société Internationale Pirelli, and then three years later its Managing Director as well. From 1982–88 he was also the Managing Director of Pirelli SpA (Milan). In 1989 Jacopo Vittorelli left those managerial positions and became Deputy Chairman of the international Pirelli Group, a position he held until his retirement in June 1993.

Dr Gavino Manca is General Manager of Economic Affairs for the Pirelli Group. A university lecturer in Economics and Business Administration at the start of his career, Dr Manca is now also Deputy Chairman of the Association of Companies in the Lombardy region, Deputy Chairman of the publishing company Il Sole 24 Ore, a member of the Board of Milan's Università degli Study, and a committee member of various cultural and scientific associations.

Silvia Petocchi is Pirelli's Corporate Human Resources Manager. Born in 1960 in Italy, she studied business administration in Milan and began her career in Minneapolis for a US-owned multinational. In 1986 she joined Pirelli as HR Development Assistant. She was then put in charge of implementing programmes in the Group's affiliates worldwide, and was appointed to her current post in 1991. Sylvia Petocchi is single and enjoys travelling, literature and sailing as her leisure pursuits.

Profilo Group — Jak V Kamhi

The Profilo Group is a holding company based in Turkey, and is one of the country's leading industrial groups, with 8000 employees worldwide. Its main sectors of activity are electronics and durable goods, and in 1992 it had an annual turnover of $635 million.

Jak V Kamhi is Chairman of the Board of the Profilo Group. Born and educated in Turkey, after university he went to France for studies in steel construction. He has set up in Turkey pilot high-tech industries in aluminium, steel production and metallic goods. He considers his profession to be his hobby, and devotes all his spare time to the study of technology research.

Among his many other activities, Jak Kamhi is one of the founders of the Union of Metal Goods Producers and remains a member of its executive committee.

Royal Dutch Shell — Ernest Van Mourik Broekman

Royal Dutch Shell has interests in more than 100 countries, operating in oil, natural gas, chemicals, metals and coal with activities in exploration, production, trading, supply, marketing, distribution and marine transport. The Group is served by headquarters in both The Hague and London, and has 130,000 staff worldwide. In 1992 the Group had an annual turnover of $100 billion.

Ernest Van Mourik Broekman is Co-ordinator of Human Resources and Organization for Shell International Petroleum. Born in South Africa, he joined Shell in 1963 and spent a good part of his career in marketing, with additional assignments in natural gas, metals and manufacturing. He is married, has two daughters and one son, and enjoys golf and opera as his leisure interests.

Saint-Gobain — Jean-Louis Beffa

Saint-Gobain is a world leader in engineering materials, with activities in flat glass, paper and wood, insulation and reinforcement, containers, pipes, ceramics and abrasives, and building materials. Started nearly 150 years ago, the company now has industrial units and subsidiaries in more than ten countries, as well as operations in a further 25 countries. In 1992 Saint-Gobain had a worldwide workforce of 105,000 employees and a turnover of FF75 billion.

Jean-Louis Beffa is Chairman and CEO of Saint-Gobain. Born in Nice in 1941, he holds degrees from the Ecole Polytechnique, Ecole Nationale Supérieure du Pétrole, and the Paris Institut d'Etudes Politiques. He began his career in the oil division of the French Ministry of Industry and in 1974 joined Saint-Gobain as Vice President for Corporate Planning. Three years later he became Managing Director and then Chairman and CEO of Pont-à-Mousson, a major subsidiary of the Saint-Gobain group. He was named CEO of the Group in 1982 and was appointed to his present position in 1986. Jean-Louis Beffa also serves on the Boards and Advisory Councils of five other international companies.

Groupe Schneider — Didier Pineau-Valencienne, Didier Guibert
Groupe Schneider operates worldwide in the areas of electrical distribution, industrial control and electrical contracting. The Group has 95,000 employees and in 1992 has a turnover of FF 61.4 billion.

Didier Pineau-Valencienne is CEO of Groupe Schneider. A graduate from l'Ecole des Hautes Etudes Commerciales and the Harvard Business School, he began his career in finance and then turned to industry in 1968, when he became Président Directeur-Général of Carbonisation et Charbons Actifs. Six years later he joined Rhône-Poulenc as Director-General of the Group's Chemical operations and became a member of the Executive Committee. In January 1981, he was named Vice-Président-Directeur Général of the Schneider Group, and the following month became its Chief Executive Officer.

Didier Pineau-Valencienne also sits on the boards of seven other international companies, three universities, and INSEAD's International Advisory Board, is President of the Institut de l'Enterprise, and is a member of the Advisory Council of the Banque de France.

Didier Guibert is Senior Vice President of Human Resources for Groupe Schneider. A graduate in Psychology, his entire career has focused on Human Resources. He first joined the Group as Vice President of Human Resources of its French subsidiary, and was appointed to his present post in 1989. He also participates in the management of many associations related to education, international mobility and adoption. Married with three children, Didier Guibert enjoys music, particularly Mozart.

Siemens AG — Walter Schusser, Hans-Jörg Hörger

Siemens' sectors of activity are power generation and transmission, defence electronics, transport and communication systems, computers, and medical engineering. The company has its headquarters in Munich. In 1992 its worldwide workforce was 390,000 and its annual turnover was DM90 billion.

Walter Schusser is Vice-President of Human Resources Management and Development in Siemens' corporate headquarters. Born in 1943, he studied economics and social sciences, and obtained his doctorate in Nuremberg, where he was first employed as a scientist at the Institute for Empirical Sociology. Since joining Siemens in 1970, he has held positions in strategic planning, business administration and industrial relations, as well as human resources. Walter Schusser is married, has two sons and likes to cycle, ski and play golf and tennis with his family.

Hans-Jörg Hörger is Executive Director of Corporate Management Training and Advanced Vocational Training. He was born in Berlin in 1935, studied electrical engineering in Stuttgart and joined Siemens in 1961. His career with the company began in research and development, but after some years he moved into human resources. He has concentrated on HR issues ever since, with a special emphasis on management education and development. Hans-Jörg Hörger is married, has two children, and loves to travel, take an active part in sports and listen to music.

Société Générale de Belgique — Viscount Etienne Davignon
Société Générale de Belgique is the largest holding company in Belgium. Founded more than 170 years ago, the Group today comprises eight companies with centres of operations in 50 countries in services, non-ferrous metals, materials and engineering, and financial services. The Group has 202,500 employees worldwide and in 1992 had a turnover of BF196 billion.

Viscount Etienne Davignon is Chairman of Société Générale de Belgique SA. He joined the company in 1985 and was appointed to his current position in 1989. Before that he had spent his career in national and international civil service.

From 1959 to 1977, Viscount Davignon was in the Belgian Ministry of Foreign Affairs, where he was Head of the Cabinets of Ministers Spaak and Harmel and then was responsible for the Political Department. After leaving the Ministry, Viscount Davignon was appointed Vice President of the Commission of the European Community in charge of industry, research and energy. During this period, he was active in the restructuring of European industry in steel, textiles and synthetic fibres and promoting new research cooperation ventures in information technology and telecommunications.

Viscount Davignon, who holds a doctorate in law, was born in Budapest, Hungary. He is married with three children.

Solvay SA — Baron Daniel Janssen

Solvay SA manufactures chemicals, plastics and health products. The company was founded in 1863 in Couillet, Belgium, by Ernest Solvay when he discovered a new and revolutionary ammonia process for the production of soda ash. Today the Solvay Group has 433 sites in 39 countries, with a worldwide workforce of 45,350. The annual turnover of the Group in 1992 was BF254.5 billion.

Baron Daniel Janssen is Chairman of the Executive Committee of Solvay. Born in Brussels, he was educated there and at Harvard University, earning degrees in civil engineering and nuclear physics, as well as an MBA. During his career he has worked with Euratom, chemical and pharmaceutical firms, lectured at universities, and served on the boards of directors of many scientific, industrial, academic and public policy councils. He joined the Board and Executive Committee of Solvay in 1984 and was appointed to his present position in 1986.

Telefónica de España — José-Alberto Blanco Losada

Telefónica de España is a telecommunications company with 74,500 employees worldwide and a turnover in 1992 of Ptas1.15 billion.

José-Alberto Blanco Losada is Deputy General Director for Strategic Planning. After graduating in economics from university in Madrid, he held several posts in that field with the Spanish Government. He joined Telefónica as an expert in 1989 and was appointed to his current position the following year.

José-Alberto Blanco Losada is married and enjoys reading, the cinema and golf as his leisure pursuits.

Titan Cement Company — Theodore Papalexopoulos
In addition to cement, the Titan Cement Company is active in ready-mixed concrete, mining, transport and shipping. Based in Athens, the company has 1545 employees and in 1992 had an annual turnover of Dr54 billion.

Theodore Papalexopoulos is Deputy Chairman of the company.

Total — Elisabeth Bukspan
The Total Group produces oil and petroleum products. It has 50,000 employees worldwide and in 1992 had an annual turnover of FF137 billion.

Elisabeth Bukspan is Director of External Affairs for the Total Group. After receiving her diploma from the Ecole Nationale d'Administration in 1975, she joined the French civil service, working first as an Inspecteur Général des Finances, then as Head of Unit in the Ministry of the Finance, and then as a special assistant to two Ministers of Trade. She moved into the private sector in 1983 as Director-General of Actim, and four years later became Secretary-General of Thomson Finance. During her period there, she was also President of ADFICAP, the French society of life insurance companies. She joined the Total Group in 1990.

Elisabeth Bukspan is also a Chevalier in the national Order of Merit.

Trafalgar House — Brian Goldthorp

Trafalgar House is among the world's top three companies in engineering and construction. In addition to those activities the Group is involved in property, shipping and hotels. With headquarters in London, Trafalgar House has 40,000 employees worldwide and in 1992 had a turnover of £3.9 billion.

Brian Goldthorp is Director of Personnel for the Trafalgar House Engineering Division, a post he has held since 1977. Before that he worked for an international management consultancy company, after earning Master's degrees in both law and psychology. Brian Goldthorp now specializes in leadership development and team building, and lectures extensively on these subjects at business schools in Europe and the United States.

Unilever — Floris A. Maljers

Unilever — one of the world's largest companies — produces foods, detergents, personal products, and speciality chemicals. Founded in 1930, Unilever's two parent companies are based in London and Rotterdam and operate as a single entity. The Group has a total of 283,000 employees worldwide and several hundred operating companies located in more than 80 countries. In 1992 Unilever had a turnover of US$44 billion.

Floris A Maljers is Chairman of the Board of Unilever. A native of the Netherlands, he joined Unilever at the age of 26 in a marketing/sales function, after having completed his studies of politics and economics in Amsterdam. Fifteen years later, in 1974, he became a member of the Board. In 1982 he became part of a three-man Chief Executive of the group, and two years later was named Chairman of the Board.

Floris Maljers is married with two sons.

Volvo — Pehr Gyllenhammar
Volvo's main areas of interest are passenger cars, trucks, buses, aerospace technology, and marine and industrial engines. One of the largest industrial groups in northern Europe, Volvo began operation in Sweden more than 60 years ago. Today it has production facilities throughout the European Community, in the United States and in South America, bringing its number of employees worldwide to 60,600. In 1992 the Group's annual turnover was Skr83 billion.

Pehr Gyllenhammar is the former Executive Chairman of Volvo, a position he held from 1990–94. He joined the company in 1970 and the following year was named Managing Director and Chief Executive Officer. In 1983 he became Chairman of the Board and CEO. As a young man, Pehr Gyllenhammar studied law at Lund University in Sweden, international law in England, and maritime law in the United States.

Pehr Gyllenhammar is married and has four children. He is a world-class sailor and is also Chairman of the Board of the Swedish Equestrian Federation.

269019